HOOKED
ON BASS

Mike and Alan relax with an 8½lb fish which took Mike's peeler crab in shallow water over rough ground.

HOOKED ON BASS

**Alan Vaughan
and Mike Ladle**

The Crowood Press

First published in 1988 by
The Crowood Press Ltd
Ramsbury, Marlborough
Wiltshire SN8 2HR

www.crowood.com

New edition 2003

British Library Cataloguing-in-Publication Data
A catalogue record for this book is available
from the British Library.

ISBN 1 86126 629 4

Acknowledgements

We wish to thank Dave Cooling, Dave Williams, Martin
Williams and Phil Williams for reading the original
manuscript; Terry Gledhill for supplying a number of
photographs; and Ian Farr for preparing black and white
prints. Lesley Vaughan deciphered our scrawl and typed the
final draft. We are also grateful to all those anglers who
supplied us with valuable information.

Typeset by Qualitext Typesetting, Abingdon
Printed in Great Britain by
Bookcraft, Midsomer Norton

Contents

Preface

The plug landed twenty yards out in the seething waves and, as it hit the water, it was seized violently. The clutch whined and line was torn from the spool as the bass ran out to sea. The 8½lb fish fought with great speed and power, making full use of the strong current and the surging undertow. Dave appeared at my side as I slid my catch on to the flat, wet rocks, an event which we repeated no less than forty-seven times in the next two hours.

I rushed along the beach to see the magnificent bass that Phil had just beached. He weighed it and the balance went down to 10½lb. With trembling fingers I baited up with a large soft edible crab and cast out. I felt a slight twitch on the line and gave some slack; the line was taken up and a pull began to develop. I struck and the rod bent right over as line was taken against the clutch. This fish pulled harder than any bass I had yet caught and, when it eventually lay beaten at the edge of the ledge, it looked enormous. Phil lifted it ashore and we weighed it swiftly: 12¼lb. Two double-figure bass in fifteen minutes – fantastic!

This book is about catching bass from the shore. When we first spoke to each other – by telephone – it was to discuss something that Mike had written on the subject of bass angling. Without having met we agreed, almost without discussion, to write this book. It is based on the many letters which we wrote to each other, edited and expanded where necessary.

Introduction

When reading angling books it is often difficult to form any impression of the author's character and experience. We thought that a thumbnail sketch of each of us, in terms of our bassing careers, might help to fill this gap.

ALAN VAUGHAN

I caught my first bass when I was seven years old from the pier at Ryde on the Isle of Wight. My father had already taken me fishing several times in a dinghy from the local angling club, and on this occasion I was using a rod he had made for me, expressly for fishing from the pier. In retrospect I realise that at the time my father was rather progressive in his attitude to fishing in the sea. Perhaps this was because of his experiences catching roach and trout in fresh water. The greenheart rods he made were not the heavy, stiff monstrosities now seen in the junk shops of most seaside towns, but they were slim and flexible and more like a modern-day spinning rod.

The small centre-pin reel had a braided line and the weight was a little spiral lead fixed some two feet from the hook, which was baited with ragworm. The worm was dangled underneath the pier at a point where the fish were known to lie and, whilst holding the rod, I had felt a pull and then caught a small bass of half a pound or so. We were fishing at night and, in the light of the lamps along the pier, my fish seemed such a glittering prize. A relatively late return home (for a seven-year-old) gave me the opportunity to show my fish to my mother and grandparents for their approval. I think that from that time on I have regarded bass as one of the most beautiful fish in the sea, and the fish I have most wanted to catch.

Since then I have fished for and caught many different fish, but always bass have been my number one obsession. I caught a lot of small bass when I was a boy and, as I read widely about angling during my teens, I became keener and keener to catch a bass of over ten pounds in weight; I have now realised that ambition several times. A good-sized bass is not only one of the most attractive and hardest-fighting fish, but has the added merit of being an excellent table fish. Large bass are not often easy to catch, so there is always a justifiable feeling of elation when a sizeable fish is brought ashore. These days, in the light of declining stocks, I also experience a great deal of satisfaction in returning bass to the sea to swim free again.

Since my days of worm dangling on the Isle of Wight, I have learned a lot about methods of catching bass. My efforts have mainly been directed towards the bigger fish so I have had only fleeting acquaintance with methods more suitable for the smaller specimens. Rarely these days do I fish the type of place where most fish are likely to be on the small side. On the whole most of my bass-fishing seasons have been spent fishing rough-ground areas by legering, usually with large crab or fish baits. I have landed many good fish, including ten to date which weighed over 10lb, the biggest at 12lb 14oz. These fish came from different places on the Welsh coast, from the Isle of Wight and from Devon, Cornwall and Eire. All of them were caught from the shore, and the methods used to catch them were comparatively simple. However, to catch good bass regularly a certain amount of single-mindedness is required, as well as a willingness to learn by one's experiences; and, of course, at least initially, a decent helping of luck is useful.

The good news about catching big bass is that anyone who can cast twenty yards (not a hundred and twenty), who is willing to approach the business with an open mind and who has a moderate degree of patience, can succeed. If the hours that a typical sea angler clocks up during the year are assessed in terms of fish caught, then he might do better to go prepared for a few blanks and expecting to lose a bit of tackle, in order to feel confident that when the big fish comes along he is doing the right thing to catch it. This has been my philosophy for a number of years now and I always feel that, at any moment, a huge fish may take my bait. This is no different perhaps from the anticipation experienced by other anglers, but I know now from past experience that I am doing the right things and that big bass are not always so scarce. If

An eight-pounder in peak condition.

the right time, place and tactics are chosen it is possible to take several big fish in a session. During one, exceptional, fortnight I caught eighteen bass with an average weight of over 8lb, including three fish in double figures.

MIKE LADLE

Unlike Alan I am not a born-and-bred bass angler. The first bass I ever caught was during my late teens. Six of us, three youths and three girls, all from the north-east of England, had decided to spend the last weeks of our summer holiday touring the country. In fact, touring is much too grand a word; we lived in a couple of ragged tents and moved from site to site in an old wreck of a car.

One of our stop-overs was at the beautiful little fishing village of St Ives in Cornwall. As always, my first stroll after setting up the camp was down to the sea. On a stone jetty I found a weather-beaten old man dressed in a navy blue jumper and crouching beside his fishing rod. As I approached he struck and reeled in a bright, silver fish of about three pounds. Although I had never seen one before, the captive was, unmistakably, a bass. My eyes devoured every detail of the old fellow's tackle – the large pierced bullet, the three-foot trace, the long-shanked, wide-gaped hook and the plump six-inch sandeel still protruding from the jaws of the fish.

I struck up a conversation, as anglers do, and as a result was presented with a couple of sandeels for my own use. Within ten minutes I had collected my little solid-glass spinning rod and, with a rig identical to that of my new friend, I was casting out my bait from a stance twenty yards beyond his. To cut a long story short, I caught a single bass, a little smaller than the one I had first seen. I was firmly hooked by the gentle bite, the racing fight and the powerful, muscular, squirming silver body as I grasped the fish, removed the hook and returned my prize to the sea. No real angler could have resisted such a drama.

When I eventually moved to the south of England in 1965, bass became reasonably common catches for me but, in general, they were small fish (less than 3lb) and were taken by accident when fishing with worm baits for flounder or pouting.

The subsequent development of my bass-fishing experience is described in some detail in the book *Operation Sea Angler*. The essence of the story is the way in which, with the help of a few good pals, I explored (perhaps I should say 'rediscovered') the use of spinning methods to catch bass from the shore. The great breakthrough, as far as I was concerned, was the use of floating jointed plugs in shallow water over rough and snaggy ground.

On plugs, my mates and I have now caught bass of all sizes up to 12½lb. Despite now having landed hundreds of good bass I still look on any of these fish as beauties. I never tire of the heart-stopping thrill which attends the violent take of a bass on my lure.

As far back as I can now remember, most seasons have been blessed with at least some fish of over 8lb. On several occasions a number of fish between 8 and 10lb have been caught in quick succession on a single trip but a double-figure bass will always represent a red-letter day.

Most of my bass fishing sessions nowadays are of pretty short duration. By picking times and places carefully it is often possible, between May and November, to catch fish on the majority of trips, even fishing on average twice a week. As in any form of fishing, there is no magic formula for success. To catch fish consistently it is necessary to be adaptable. Although artificial lures are the mainstay of my approach, I am always prepared, when it is

Flat Ledge – which accelerates the longshore currents and holds bass.

appropriate, to leger, float-fish or fly-fish with baits ranging from crab to maggots and from livebait to worms. My philosophy of bass angling can be expressed quite simply as 'Look before you think and think before you fish'.

1

The Life Cycle of the Bass

The bass is a fish of slow growth. It attains a fairly large average size only because it appears to have a much longer 'expectation of life' than the generality of sea fishes.

Michael Kennedy, *The Sea Angler's Fishes*, 1954

ML   In the clear, cold waters of the English Channel, the first hint of the spring bloom of microscopic plants was staining the sea with a translucent, greenish tinge. The surface of the sea, untroubled by wind or rain, was swelling gently into deep oily dunes of water as it rounded the rugged, cliff-bound peninsula. As the tide began to flood towards the east, powerful eddies and surges broke upwards from the seabed pinnacles to boil on the surface of the race.

Half a mile north of the lighthouse, perched like a sentinel on the prominent rock, and twenty feet beneath the rolling swell, a school of grey-backed, silver-sided fish stemmed the powerful flow, seemingly with no effort. All the fish in the school were thickset male bass in the prime of life. The largest of them was over 8lb, but the majority were small fish of less than 4lb; all were now in breeding condition.

It was now the first week in May and the water was warm for the time of year. This followed a mild spell of weather which had lasted since Christmas. The male bass had been shoaled up, patiently waiting in the tide race, for almost two weeks. They fed, when the opportunity arose, on scattered shoals of tiny sandeels.

Suddenly a sense of excitement rippled through the assembled fish as a group of grey shapes loomed up from below. The largest of these newcomers was well into double figures and their flanks bulged with eggs, accumulated in the summer of the previous year. The excitement rose as the females entered the shoal and the male

12

fish jostled and pressed around them, mouths agape and bodies quivering as their milt was released. Streams of tiny amber eggs issued from the hen fish and most of them were fertilised as they dispersed and drifted slowly up towards the surface of the sea. As quickly and as silently as they had arrived, the larger bass disappeared and the shoal of males settled once more to their silent wait.

In the following four or five days the fertilised eggs were carried to and fro on the tidal streams. Many of them became suspended in the cycling currents over the banks of shell-grit which lay on either side of the race. The vulnerable microscopic amber beads fell prey to a host of tiny, transparent, pulsing jellyfish, bristly, twitching copepods, fierce, spiky crab larvae and the fry of lesser fish such as rocklings. As the eggs drifted, they developed within them muscles, bones, nerves and little black eyes. By early June the tiny fish were visible, curled tightly inside their protective membranes.

As the bass larvae, each sporting a little sac of yolk, burst from their eggs, the fluid released by their escape attracted a further host of mini-predators. The stinging, thread-like tentacles of jellyfish entrapped countless young fish. Others fell victim to the shimmering comb-jellies. Glued to the branching, trailing, elastic filaments of the predators they were, one after another, reeled in and stuffed into wide-stretched mouths. Within the transparent bodies of the comb-jellies they joined their fellows, already crammed like little sardines, inside the bulging guts of their captors. Arrow worms, like vibrant slivers of glass, bristling with sickle-shaped jaws, lanced into the huddles of baby fish.

The surviving bass larvae were almost capable of swimming now, feeding on tiny pinpoints of marine life, too small and slow to escape even their feeble movements. Those which were lucky enough to encounter rich patches of food were growing quickly. Others, less fortunate, starved or died of disease. Four weeks after hatching many of them were swept close inshore by warm onshore breezes, in through the stone-flanked mouth of the harbour and into the torrent of salt water flowing in the narrow channel which led into a huge, shallow lagoon beyond. As they were swept along in the strong flow, many of them fell prey to the clumsy lunges of last year's young pollack.

The most advanced larvae were already developing tiny scales as they swam about in tight little shoals over the shallow, eel-grass-clothed mud flats. The smaller specimens were mopped up by hordes of greedy gobies, with pop-eyes and rubber-lipped mouths, always on the look-out for an easy meal. The surface of the mud was a meshwork of lethal tentacles fringing the discs of burrowing anemones. Along with the bass, young sand-smelts and mullet were trapped, stung and swallowed.

As midsummer came and went the shallows warmed up, reaching 25° or 30°C on the hot sunny days. The young bass, now over an inch in length, prepared actively for the coming winter by consuming countless mysid shrimps, beach fleas and other small crustaceans, on which they pounced with typical bass-like ferocity. As they grew bigger, their diet changed to include larger marine slaters and burrowing sandhoppers (*Corophium*), which lived in little U-shaped tunnels near the high water mark.

The young bass spent their first winter in tidal channels sculpted by the run-off of water from the mud flats. In the next couple of years they fed, and grew fat, on the ragworms, crustaceans and midge larvae (bloodworms) swarming in their countless millions on the rotting eel-grasses which represented the rich, organic crop of the lagoon.

Some of the young fish had the good fortune to inhabit areas where the natural heat of the sun was supplemented by a flow of warm water from the cooling system of a power station. Even in winter, when ice fringed the mud flats, these lucky little bass continued to feed and grow more or less throughout the cold season, becoming nearly double the size of their siblings by the following year.

The power-station outfall, with its strong-flowing sources of heated salt water, provided the school bass with an almost ideal place to live. Injured and helpless prey animals, drifting along in the swift flow, were easy meat for the streamlined little predators. Boulders introduced to absorb the energy of the flowing water provided a haven for small shrimps, prawns, sandhoppers and slaters, which the bass nosed out and devoured. The warm water encouraged settlement of drifting larvae and enhanced the growth of ragworms, 'snails', crabs and similar prey. Bass of three or four inches long, now about one year old, fed very heavily on brown shrimps and mysid shrimps.

The young bass, like all young animals, were vulnerable to many predators and natural disasters. Lots of them perished when

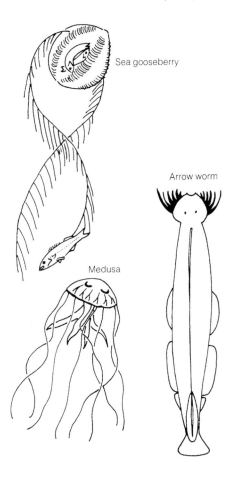

Sea gooseberry

Predatory plankton animals which take a heavy toll of tiny bass.

Arrow worm

Medusa

they were trapped on the intake screens of the power-station, particularly in the autumn, when they were close inshore. In winter many of them moved seaward so that fewer of the little fish turned up amongst the rubbish on the screens but, where temperatures were higher due to the inflows of warm water, the little fish were inclined to stay put throughout the year.

During their first years the weather had been kind and more young bass than usual had survived the vagaries of the climate and the predation of many enemies. In the following years the young bass devoted their energies to feeding and growing. Then, between the ages of five and six, when they were just over one foot in length, the male fish became mature. The females matured when they were a little older and a little larger, perhaps fifteen inches in

The opercular (gill cover) bone of a sixteen-year-old, 7½lb bass.

Scales from a bass caught in 1985. The fish was spawned in 1976 and nine annuli (annual rings) can be clearly seen.

length and seven years of age. After they reached maturity the fish bred every year and in every spawning season each female laid her eggs in several batches.

After spawning, the adult fish fed actively throughout the summer and autumn months, until shortening days and falling water temperatures drove them to migrate towards the south and west and to settle for the winter in offshore resting areas until increasing day length and rising temperatures stirred them into another cycle of migration, breeding and feeding.

This then is the life of the bass, as we understand it at present. In British and Irish waters their feeding and growing season is quite short and, as a result, it will probably take twenty years for a female fish to reach a weight in double figures; male bass are slightly slower-growing and rarely exceed 8lb in weight. In warmer waters off the French coast growth rates are similar, but further south, along the Atlantic coast of Morocco, a fish of 10lb will typically be only twelve or thirteen years old. On a day-to-day basis sea temperature is important in the way it affects feeding activity and, consequently, the growth of bass.

The history of every individual fish is recorded in its scales and bones. The principle is exactly the same as the well-known method of counting the rings in tree trunks to read the age of the tree. Not only do the number of rings (annuli) allow us to estimate the age of a fish, but there is much more we can learn from bass scales.

It is worth saying a word or two about the growth of scales themselves. When a young bass hatches from its egg it has no scales, and it is only a month or so later that the armour plating begins to develop. The first tiny scales appear on the flank, just by the tip of the pectoral fin, so these are the oldest scales and therefore the best guide to the age of the fish. As a bass goes through its life it gets knocked about by waves, rocks, predators, territorial battles or encounters with nets, anglers and other hazards. These scraps and scrapes may dislodge scales from the body. When new, replacement, scales grow to patch up the damaged areas they have no rings in the central zone, which looks distinctly rough and fuzzy. Such 'repair' scales cannot, of course, give a full record of the fish's age, so several scales are needed from each bass to ensure that one or two good ones are obtained for reading.

Not only do scales reveal the age of a bass, but in warm summers when food is plentiful, the fish and its scales will grow quickly, producing a wide space between successive rings.

Following a bad year, of course, the rings will be close together. The edge of the scale represents the time when the fish was caught so, by working back towards the centre, it is possible to determine how much the bass grew in each year of its life. All fish and scales grow a little less in length with each succeeding year, so the spacing of rings near the edge of the scale will always be much less than near the centre.

So what? When you are sitting it out and waiting for a bass to take your carefully placed and presented peeler crab, *does it matter* how quickly the fish which you are not catching grew five years ago – or, indeed, at any stage in its life? Perhaps not, although it is interesting to look at scales, or alternatively the bones of the gill cover (operculum), of a particularly plump or emaciated fish to check on its recent growth.

Much more important than just satisfying the angler's curiosity, is the scientific value of the accumulated knowledge from scale readings of many fish. It soon becomes obvious that fish born in a particular year are more abundant than those born in other years. From this it is clear that the number of recruits (survivors of the year's crop of eggs) is occasionally much greater than usual. In fact the bass in British waters, because it is at the northern limit of its range, often has spawning failures and only when everything comes together do we see a strong year class.

Just as in the case of the American striped bass, all the evidence suggests that our bass stocks are in overall decline. However, this decline can be temporarily reversed by an unusually successful breeding season. One such successful year was 1959, and an exceptional number of bass were spawned and survived from that season. These fish then provided sport for about twenty years, though unfortunately they are likely to be all but vanished now. 1949 was another very good year. We can but hope for more years like these, and when they arrive, we must take every opportunity to protect and conserve these beautiful fish so that our children and grandchildren can enjoy them as we do.

2
Food

If the bass are feeding on 1½-inch whitebait I do not expect them to take readily a 3-inch artificial.

P. Wadham, *B.S.A.S. Quarterly,* 1921

ML The baits used for bass are well known, so why bother to look at what bass normally eat? There are several good reasons for this. First, by knowing where and when particular foods are likely to be available, we can choose the best bait and presentation for each fishing session. Second, there is no doubt that conventional baits and lures have limitations and the basis for improvements has to be in the natural diet of the fish. Last, in selecting venues, fishing spots, positions and even stances, a knowledge of the basic behaviour of food items can be invaluable.

Table 1 lists bass stomach contents as recorded by several different anglers. These lists show better than any other information how bass change their feeding habits from one place to another. After a look at what the fish actually eat, a short description of the natural history of many of these creatures should help us to decide where and when the bass will expect to find them.

Before we go on to consider the tables, bear in mind that an angler using a particular bait is to some extent selecting fish which are hunting for that type of food. Despite this problem, there can be little doubt that the bass in different places are accustomed to eating different proportions of the various food items.

There will also be a certain amount of geographical variation in the type of food available. A fish which is patrolling the north-western limits of bass distribution along the coast of Lancashire or Cumbria will not encounter the same variety of edible animals as one around the rocks of Land's End or one at the other extreme of decent bass fishing in the southern North Sea.

The picture which emerges from Table 1 is tricky to understand.

Table 1   Stomach Contents of Rod-caught Bass

Isle of Wight		Isle of Wight		Dorset		North Cornwall	
77 bass		79 bass		88 bass		87 bass	
Angler: B. Warne		*Angler:* A. Vaughan		*Angler:* M. Ladle		*Investigator:*	
Bait: Fish or cuttle		*Bait:* 50/50		*Bait:* Plug		D. Kelley	
Empty	31	Crab/Fish		Empty	34	*Bait:* —	
Crab	34	Empty	12	Shore crab	17	Crab	55
Fish	16	Shore crab	37	Swimming crab	6	Sandeel	26
Cuttlefish	14	Edible crab	3	Edible crab	5	Prawn/Shrimp	12
Shrimp	1	Spider crab	2	Spider crab	2	Other items were:	
		Squat lobster	2	Xantho crab	1	Fish	
		Fish	41	Fish	12	Octopus	
		Shrimp	3	Shrimp	2	Squid	
		Ragworm	4	Prawn	1	Lugworm	
		Limpet	1	Ragworm	2	Hopper	
		Egg mass	1	Top shell	1	Slater	
				Limpet	1		
				Hopper	1		
				Algae	2		
				Maggots	19		
				Bird	1		

SW Ireland		Menai Straits		Menai Straits	
103 bass		61 bass		53 bass	
Investigator: M. Kennedy		*Angler:* A. Vaughan		*Investigator:* E. Tan	
Bait:—		*Bait:* Crab		*Bait:*—	
Empty	11	Empty	11	Empty	—
Shore crab	61	Shore crab	24	Shore crab	30
Edible crab	3	Edible crab	27	Edible crab	24
Swimming crab	2	Fish	11	Fish	15
Hermit crab	2	Shrimp	7	Shrimp	8
Fish	39	Ragworm	1	Ragworm	1
Shrimp	22	Lugworm	1	Lugworm	2
Prawn	6	Barnacle	1		
Lugworm	3				
Slater	8				
Bivalve	2				
Anemone	1				

The numbers show how many bass contained each type of food.

Other samples of fish from the Dorset coast showed that occasionally the bass had been feeding intensively on a single type of food. At times, sea slaters were the only food present in dozens of fish caught. Kennedy and Fitzmaurice give an extensive list of bass gut contents from south-west Ireland. Shore crabs were noted to be the most abundant items and, apart from a wide range of fish species, hermit crab, swimming crab, shrimp, prawn, slater, squid, cuttlefish and octopus were recorded from the stomachs of the Irish bass.

Crabs, of various sorts, are *always* well represented in bass food and obviously they are important. However, crabs are pretty tough, shelly creatures and may resist digestion for quite a time. There are no studies on bass digestion, but scientists working on other species of fish have shown that crab may last several times as long as fish in the acids and enzymes of a fish's stomach. So it is quite likely that more fish are actually eaten than the table suggests – perhaps at least as many fish are eaten as crabs in most cases. By the same reasoning, other soft foods like worms may be a bit more popular with the bass than they seem.

Although crabs and fish make up the bulk of a bass's diet, there are quite striking differences in detail. In the Menai Straits edible crabs loom large; in south-west Ireland, Cornwall and the Isle of Wight shore crabs were the main crustaceans; while in south Dorset, although shore crabs were abundant, edible and velvet swimming crabs were also very well represented.

Whereas in Cornwall sandeels were the main fish eaten, in other places different species predominated – wrasse in the Isle of Wight, flatfish in the Menai Straits and south-west Ireland and a wide range, including rockling, pipefish and sea trout in south Dorset (*see* Table 2, page 25).

In addition to these major foodstuffs, there are some surprising

Above left: edible crab. Above right: velvet swimming crab.
Below: shore crab. These are the most useful crabs for bait.

features. In Dorset maggots (of the seaweed fly) were often eaten in large quantities. In Cornwall sandhoppers were consumed by a fair number of the bass examined. In the Isle of Wight cuttlefish were sometimes important and in the Menai Straits and south-west Ireland shrimps and prawns were eaten. In Dorset and south-west Ireland slaters fell prey to the bass in great numbers.

Obviously, the larger bass eat other fish and various crabs when they can get hold of them and this should be (and is) the basis of most of our fishing methods. However, bass are clearly opportunists in the sense that if *any* sort of creature becomes available in large quantities they switch on to that food. The really successful bass angler must also be prepared to switch when he needs to – whether the groundbait is natural, such as maggots, slaters or hoppers, or less natural, such as fish offal, bread or cheese.

CRABS

Hard crabs are the items most frequently found in the guts of decent-sized bass. Although these crusty mouthfuls are good baits for wrasse (ballan and corkwing), and are often used for this purpose, few bass are caught on them. Frequently bass must be present in the areas where anglers are fishing for wrasse with hard-crab baits, but rarely, if ever, do they seem to have a go.

Crabs eaten by bass include the well-known shore crab (*Carcinus maenas*), the edible crab (*Cancer pagurus*) and the velvet swimming crab (*Liocarcinus puber*). These are by no means the only crustaceans which bass find tasty. The list is quite long. Small swimming crabs (*Macropipus depurator*), which are often abundant in offshore sandy areas, frequently occur in guts. Burrowing masked crabs (*Corystes*), squat lobsters, sea slaters, spider crabs, prawns, shrimps, lobsters and hermit crabs are also eaten by bass from time to time.

Why then should soft or peeler crabs be such outstanding baits? All crustaceans grow by moulting their shells when these become small and cramped. Moulting or 'peeling' occurs more frequently when they are young, when the weather is warm, before they are due to mate (males) and at mating time (females). At all of these times the crabs will be extra vulnerable because, for various periods:

1. They will be inactive (easier to catch).
2. They will be less aggressive (easier to deal with).
3. They will release 'moulting fluids' (be easier to smell).
4. The new (soft) shell will leak (be easier to smell).

Mature crabs can mate only when the females are soft-shelled. Many species have a rather short breeding season, when peeling and soft females are plentiful.

The pattern Alan has noticed each year when collecting shore crabs is that in April and May there is an increase in the number found and most of them are males; shortly afterwards they peel. Later on in May or June the females appear and peel. Then many pairs of crabs are present, making bait gathering easier. At this time it is rather unusual to find females unattended by males, unless they are carrying eggs. As the season progresses, crabs of both sexes are found separately on the shore and some may be peeling or soft. There seems to be a second peeling season for male shore crabs at the end of the summer (late August and September) on some stretches of coastline.

Although *young* shore crabs probably moult several times each year, the mature animals shed their shells only once annually, living for five or six years. It seems likely that males are attracted to females by some chemical attractant, but so far scientists have been unable to detect one. Some moulting shore crabs are usually present on the shore at any time of the year, but there are very few to be found in the winter.

Edible crabs follow a similar pattern, but the larger specimens, which migrate extensively during the year, first appear on the shore a few weeks later than the shore crabs. Again the males peel first and afterwards the females are usually the bait collector's reward throughout the summer up to September or October, depending on locality.

In south-west England in most months of the year some edible crabs will probably be moulting. Females probably shed their shells less often than males. Small (undersized) crabs, of about four inches in shell width, generally moult once a year, but as they grow older they change skins less often.

Velvet swimming crabs tend to live on more exposed rocky shores. They are often quite common under stones in the rock pools of the kelp zone. Because they live low down on the shore, they are susceptible to exposure and soon die out of water.

John Darling, fishing in Sussex, has commented on the 'synchronised' peeling of velvet swimming crabs. He suggests that plenty of peelers are available in June though peeling is restricted to rather a short period. He confirms that these crabs are first-class bass baits, even to the extent that they may work when shore crabs are almost useless. Alan has found plenty of soft and peeling velvets later in the season, but not many in June, on the beaches he has fished. One 10lb bass which he caught was absolutely crammed with soft velvet crab; this was in Devon during September, the month when he has found velvet swimmers most plentiful in 'bait condition'.

It is not surprising that anglers have long known these sizeable, soft animals to be the favoured foods of many fish. It seems that in different localities, at different times during the season, one or other species of crab will be common and peeling. At these times bass are likely to become preoccupied with feeding on crabs.

If bass are looking for crabs, they will certainly tend to search in places where their prey is abundant. The fish probably learn to anticipate the regular migrations of the crabs. For example, on mud flats in the Menai Straits, North Wales, television cameras have been used by scientists to study the tidal movements of crabs in summer. Most crabs travelled up the shore about three hours after low water, and moved down again an hour and a half before the next low water. Along every metre of the shoreline approximately 84 crabs moved up the beach on each flood tide. Peak movements took place when the water was over half a metre deep.

FISH

The picture which emerges from Table 2 is that bass will eat almost any other fish. Presumably the very striking differences between the lists show what species are most easily available in each place. One or two noteworthy points are that:

1. Sandeels are by no means the main food fish of bass everywhere.
2. Wrasse, which are certainly very common in most of the areas considered, do not often figure in the diet.

3. Other species might be expected to bulk largely but *do not* – these include pouting, poor-cod, pollack, sand-smelt and mackerel.

Table 2   Fish in the Stomach Contents of Bass

Isle of Wight	Dorset	North Cornwall	Eire
A. Vaughan	*M. Ladle*	*D. Kelley*	*M. Kennedy*
+Wrasse	+Sandeel	+Sandeel	++Flounder
Gurnard	+Pipefish	Flounder	+Sandeel
Rockling	+15-spined stickle	Mullet	+Sprat
Sandeel	+Blenny	Sprat	Butterfish
15-spined stickle	+Rockling		Blenny
Blenny	Goby		Brill
Mackerel	Dragonet		Mullet
Herring	Eel		Pollack
	Wrasse		Wrasse
			Sea trout
			15-spined stickle
North Wales			Sea scorpion
A. Vaughan			Pilchard
+Sea scorpion			Smolt
+Plaice			Plaice
+Dab			Sand-smelt
Eel			Coalfish
Butterfish			Whiting

++indicates abundant and +indicates frequent.
The exact species, size and numbers of fish eaten in each area varies from time to time. As in the case of other foods, bass sometimes feed almost exclusively on a certain fish. For example, two catches made in Dorset, which totalled almost a hundred fish, contained only sandeels, and dozens of bass had eaten only 'rock fish' (pipefishes, rocklings, blennies, etc.).

The species that the bass will be looking for differ from place to place. Broadly speaking, the shore angler will be concerned with small shore fish or with the young of inshore species. It would be impossible to deal with every species, but it is unlikely that the bass care too much whether it is a rockling, a blenny or a goby that is sliding down their throats.

Why don't bass eat more of these common species? Several of them make good baits – for example, mackerel, wrasse, pouting and sand-smelt. Presumably, for a variety of reasons, they are not usually available to the hunting bass. The pouting are, more or less, nocturnal, and by sheltering in tight shoals near the seabed

Some fish of different shapes and forms which are eaten by bass.

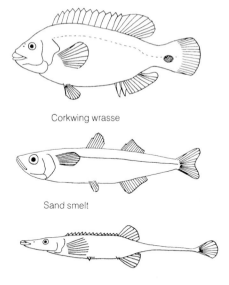

Corkwing wrasse

Sand smelt

Fifteen-spined stickleback

during the hours of daylight they may avoid foraging bass. What about the others? Small wrasse presumably retreat quickly into rocky corners and crevices at the approach of danger. Mackerel dodge attackers by high speed cruising, and by compact schooling, which is another effective anti-predator tactic. How about the sand-smelts? They are small, conspicuous, surface-swimming fish which are often abundant in the same areas as bass. In Dorset sand-smelts are often to be seen in summer and autumn ringing the water surface as they swim along. Shoal after shoal of these tasty little relatives of the mullet swim past, sometimes leaping from the water, as your lure is reeled in through their midst. Yet, for some reason 'smelts' are seldom found inside bass (except when they are someone's bait).

No one knows all the answers to the question why bass eat some fish and not others, but consideration of the most important factors may suggest where and how to use a fish bait most effectively.

The main defences of most intertidal fishes against being eaten are camouflage, alertness, agility and an intimate knowledge of their surroundings which enables them to gain refuge quickly when they are threatened. The very shallowness of the water generally gives these fish plenty of protection from being eaten by

Inshore fish eaten by bass – whiting and pouting.

Inshore fish eaten by bass – corkwing wrasse. Above: female.
Below: male.

Catching wrasse for bait by using light float tackle.

larger fish. Many predators are deterred from venturing into places where they may become stranded, so the blenny in its pool on the upper shore or the goby swimming about in a couple of inches of water over clean sand may be safe (though not, of course, from terns and gulls). If the bass is to catch these fish it must be prepared to enter shallow water. Also, there will be times when the rock- or sand-pool fish is particularly vulnerable. When a wave breaks and pounds down on to the shore, the less wary or unlucky fish may be briefly swept from its hiding place or displaced into the 'boiling' water. If the bass is to catch it, it must first be in the surf and, second, it must be quick off the mark to make its capture before the smaller fish recovers and regains the shelter of a crevice. Obviously, the rougher the sea the more likely it is to dislodge potential prey.

What will the bass be looking for? It must, if it is to feed efficiently, get its eye in and acquire a 'search image'. To do this it will be recognising particular shapes, colours and movements. Since most of the forage fish are coloured like weed, rock or sand and the bass does not want to waste time swallowing bits of weed, eel-grass or stones, then shape and – even more – movement will be what it reacts to. Could this be the key?

Table 2 shows that this shape factor will vary a lot from place to place. In a muddy estuary young flounders may be the target. In kelp-filled gullies the search image could approximate to plump, chestnut-coloured wrasse and, as the flat rocks are washed by the incoming tide, the sinuous brownish or greenish forms of blennies or rocklings may be what switch on the bass's feeding reaction. In many places the search image will become the slender silver form of the sandeels. These fish, despite their name, are free-swimming, daylight-loving, midwater fish, which spend much of their time in open water over both rocky and soft bottoms. All the sandeel species look similar in shape, colour and movement and for certain the bass eat all of them with equal relish.

RAGWORMS

There are many types of ragworm and the best known is probably the king rag (*Nereis virens*), which is widespread in sticky, stony mud. They are tough and lively worms and generally remain well hidden, making good use of sheltering rocks and ledges. At about three years old the worms breed, during spring when the water is cold (7–8°C). They begin to spawn four days after the full moon in a series of spring tides.

All the male worms leave the safety of their burrows to breed and, towards low water, many thousands of them may be swimming about in the sea above the mud flats. They are light-green in colour, turning darker as they become spent, and provide rich pickings for school bass in April and May.

The small harbour rag (*Nereis diversicolor*) lives in sand, mud or clay on the upper half of the shore. Because this species is attracted to fresh water, it is generally found in estuaries or where springs or seepages trickle through the sediment. Unlike king rag, these worms spawn from within their burrows. Harbour rag feed on particles of algae and sediment, which they pick up or filter from the water with a little net of slime. The worms may leave their holes to migrate to more favourable places and then it is that the schoolies feed on them.

Of all the species of ragworms which are eaten by fish, the orange and green worms (*Nereis pelagica*), living in rock crevices or gullies, are perhaps the most active. These muscular, writhing, glistening creatures can sometimes be seen on mild summer nights, wriggling along just beneath the calm surface of the sea like four-inch elastic bands. This habit must present a chance for anglers to experiment, after dark, with surface-fished worm baits, soft rubber lures or streamer flies.

Several species of white ragworms (*Nephthys* spp) are found in sand or muddy sand all around the shores of Britain. They are slim, glistening, off-white, plastic-like animals which can burrow quickly through hard sand by shooting out their powerful muscular 'throat'. They are all fierce predators, actively hunting small animals in the sand. They often behave as cannibals, eating smaller white ragworms. White rag may be most vulnerable in March or April when some species breed *en masse*, but they do not normally leave their burrows. They are common items of food for fish which feed over sandy seabeds. The largest species (*Nephthys caeca*), growing up to about nine inches long, is found mainly below low tide level and is therefore usually only collected by anglers digging bait on low spring tides. White ragworms are mostly long-lived animals (up to six years) and in Britain are subject to complete spawning failure in some years. Each worm may breed several times in the course of its life.

LUGWORMS

There are two common species of lugworm around our coasts: first, the tail-less lugworm (*Arenicola ecaudata*), which, as its name suggests, does not have the thinner, yellowish 'tail' end of its relative; and, second, the common lugworm (*Arenicola marina*).

The tail-less worm, little known to anglers, lives in stony, muddy beaches and is too soft for distance casting, although I have caught bass on them. Sometimes they provide a handy windfall source of bait on rocky shores because they can be found under stones in patches of muddy sand. Bass hunting over rocky gullies and ledges may eat them, particularly when they are disturbed by rough weather.

Ordinary lugworms are probably a regular source of food for bass feeding in harbours and over sandy flats and beaches. The most likely times for these animals to be available to bass are:

1. When they come to the surface to eject their casts. Each worm does this about every 40–50 minutes and the tip of its tail (at least) may then be available to an alert fish.

2. During and after heavy weather, when even the deepest burrows may be washed out and the worms injured.
3. In May when the worms migrate, by swimming, to recolonise beaches.
4. During breeding, which occurs at low tide when the air temperature is low, after the middle of October. Many of the worms then emerge from their burrows and die on the surface.
5. When the sand has been extensively disturbed by bait digging.

All these events give the bass a chance to find a meal and the angler a chance to catch the bass. They should be considered when deciding when and where to fish. One other point may be worth a mention in relation to lugworm: when the larvae of the worms settle on the shore they often choose the highest tidal levels. Small thin casts on the upper shore give way to the plump, sandy coils of adult worms further down the beach. Lug are never evenly distributed, even on flat expanses of sand. Failing any other indication of where to place my bait, I generally have a look, at low tide, to see where the casts are thickest.

SQUID, CUTTLEFISH AND OCTOPUS

With their well-developed arms and fins, powerful muscular bodies, superb sense organs and large brains, these animals are as well equipped for life in the sea as any fish. Because they are so active and alert, squid are rarely caught by fishermen or scientists and, consequently, they are poorly understood. Cuttlefish and octopus, being confined, more or less, to the seabed, are more easily trapped and netted.

There are many species of squid and cuttle in British waters but only two types of octopus (the well-known southern form, *Octopus vulgaris,* and another species, *Eledone cirrhosa;* which lives in colder northern waters). Bass will eat any and all of these animals if the chance arises, but the ones most readily available as food are the various cuttlefish near sandy seabeds and the streamlined surface-shoaling squids in deeper, more open water.

Because of their juicy, meaty bodies, all of these cephalopods are rather vulnerable to predatory fish. Their defence is based on the principles of camouflage, illusion and deterrence rather than aggression or fight-back. Most of them are translucent, rather like tinted polythene, and surface-swimming squid are often practically invisible apart from their large lustrous eyes. All of these animals are capable of rapid colour change. The actual patterns and colours depend on how the animal feels. Normally it would blend into the background of rocks, weed or sand. When threatened the animal will first try to confuse the attacker with rapid darts for cover combined with swift changes of colour. If pressed further, it may try to bluff it out with a threat. The common cuttlefish, for example, blanches white with two large black 'eyes' on the mantle. If such threats work (and presumably they are intended to startle fish such as bass) we as anglers should be wary of using lures or baits coloured in a 'threatening' fashion.

The last resort of all these species is a cloud of ink. This has several functions – it acts as a smoke screen, as a distraction, and as a nose-numbing 'nerve gas'. This last effect is important from the angler's point of view and suggests that all ink should be washed off squid or cuttle used for bait.

It is obvious from Table 1 that cuttle are occasionally eaten in quite large numbers by bass. Along sandy beaches in the south of England it is not uncommon to catch bass in which the little cuttle, a small sand-burrowing form, is present in the stomach. Off south-west Ireland both squid and octopus are also found in bass.

Squid and cuttlefish which are eaten by bass. The 'black-eye' threat display of the common cuttlefish is intended to scare off predators.

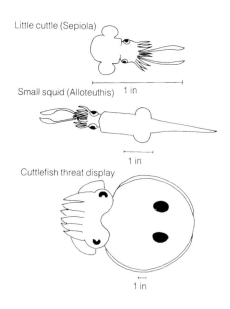

Little cuttle (Sepiola)

Small squid (Alloteuthis)   1 in

1 in

Cuttlefish threat display

1 in

Most of these molluscs are active mainly at night and, presumably, it is at night that the hunting bass expects to find them in the open. At times of mass spawning, mass migration or mass death (caused by weather conditions, for example) they are likely to be available as food in quantity, but little is known of their habits.

RAZORFISH AND CLAMS

These are two very differently shaped molluscs. In common they have the characteristic of providing a large, juicy, pale-coloured bait. Neither of them is likely to be readily available to bass, unless disturbed by heavy seas or bait diggers.

Razorfish, living as they do on more open shores than clams, are more susceptible to being washed out by the waves. Unlike clams, they are active burrowers and, unless injured, can quickly dig back into the sand using a long muscular foot as a sort of anchor-excavator.

Clams live a pretty passive existence, permanently embedded in stiff clayey sediments (for choice) and in their deep retreats they must be practically safe from storms. Once the clam reaches a decent size, its burrowing foot wastes away, becoming small and weak, so it can no longer dig into the mud. As the clam ages it gradually increases the size of its burrow and a big one may be securely lodged a foot or more down in the mud. To feed, it reaches up to the surface with its tough and leathery trunk-like siphon.

SHRIMPS AND PRAWNS

Shrimps and prawns are eaten by bass of all sizes. Both are practically defenceless when it comes to a straight contest with the marauding bass, but each has its own devices for avoiding predation.

The shrimp (*Crangon* spp) has immaculate camouflage with a fantastic pepper-and-salt shell, perfectly matching the sand over which it lives. Like many other bottom-living creatures, shrimps change colour to match the background. During the hours of daylight the shrimps dig in by shuffling their feathery legs and sweeping away the loose sand with a jet of water. This disturbance of the sand is often the only visible sign of the little crustacean and no doubt the bass are well aware of this.

Shrimps come out of the sand when roughness colours the water or at night – just as the sandeels 'go to bed' – and schoolies in particular hunt them down along the surf line just as the tide begins to flood.

Despite their fragile appearance, shrimps are among the toughest animals in the sea and can withstand almost anything except drying out. Summer and winter, in estuary and on open shore, they scud their way along the seabed. In fact it is often in the coldest part of the year that they lay their eggs and for three months the big, fat, egg-laden females provide a fine food source for those bass which brave the winter and spring in our northern waters.

Where rock and weed predominate, even though there will be shrimps on the sandy patches, various types of prawn (*Leander* spp) will dominate the scene. From the angler's point of view all prawns look alike and it is doubtful whether bass care which type they are eating.

The species usually found in rock pools is quite small (up to about two inches long) and hardly makes a decent bait. A size 8 hook is usually about the right size for these rock-pool mini-prawns. In winter the small prawns move offshore, returning to the pools in spring. Frequently there are prawns in all the pools right up to the highest tidal levels, where there may be hundreds among the slimy green filaments of algae during the summer months. In the warm weather these prawns moult every two or three weeks, but, unlike crabs, they harden the new shell quickly, so soft-shelled prawns are not vulnerable for long. After moulting, in early summer, the females carry round a couple of thousand little round eggs.

The bigger prawn (*Leander serratus*) only lives on the south and west coasts of Britain (rather like the bass). It occurs within and below the tide marks, both along the open coast and in estuaries. It may grow up to four inches long and big ones make cracking great baits. These are the prawns which are caught in pots, cooked, and sold as 'local' prawns in seaside towns.

Prawns, like shrimps, have evolved ways of life which keep them well away from marauding bass. Their main period of activity occurs on the ebbing spring tides, particularly at dawn and dusk in summer, so this is when the bass will expect to come across them. The other time when they are likely to be easy meat is when heavy seas or surging surf are crashing into shallow rock pools on the flood tide. In such conditions bass and wrasse, following the waves into the shallows, will pick up the prawns swirling in the undertow.

SLATERS AND HOPPERS

Michael Kennedy reports that bass from the Dingle Peninsula in Eire were found to contain masses of isopods (sea slaters). These fast swimming, streamlined, mahogany-coloured creatures (*Idotea* spp) often turn up in enormous numbers where quantities of wrack, kelp or other fresh but broken weed lie in the shallow water. In 1949 Don Kelley also recorded fish from North Devon with enormous numbers of 'rocklice' (slaters) in their stomachs. In the same collection were thirteen bass (mainly small) with lots of amphipods (sandhoppers) in their guts.

Big bass certainly feed on slaters when these are abundant. It is a very local business and the bass angler should learn to recognise the places where slaters will be numerous. A good description of the right conditions is given by Naylor. At Port Erin on the Isle of Man there is a ruined breakwater which forms a sheltered corner with the shore, in which damaged weed, driven in by storms, collects in the shallow water.

The slaters feed on the bits of seaweed and they can be fantastically numerous. I have lifted a ragworm bait from the water to find about four ounces of slaters clinging to it, forming a ball. As they were hoisted aloft, most of the slaters let go and the mass fell back with a plop. These slaters are active swimmers; they hurtle along with their bodies stretched out straight and their little legs kicking wildly. The bass may become totally preoccupied with them, particularly when heavy seas and coloured water disturb them. Bass feeding on slaters will sometimes take plugs, buoyant Mepps or any of the usual natural baits, but slaters on small hooks and light tackle, or 'slater flies' on trout fly gear, will probably give the best results if conditions permit. Often, when there is a heavy

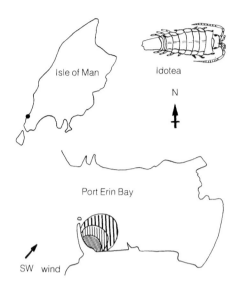

A slater corner in Port Erin Bay, Isle of Man. Fragments of loose weed accumulate in the shelter of the break-water and are colonised by vast numbers of sea slaters (Idotea spp). Large bass may become preoccupied with slaters as food.

groundswell, there are many tons of weed bits in the water. Small and big bass eat slaters, in quantity, in such situations.

Large male slaters may reach an inch in length and the females about half an inch. In summer the animals are smaller than in winter and spring. March – April and September – October are probably the best times to fish 'slater corners' with appropriate methods.

Just as they will eat slaters, bass will gorge themselves on sandhoppers. Don Kelley found more than 10 per cent of the bass which he examined in North Devon had 'uncountable' numbers of sandhoppers in their guts.

Whenever possible sandhoppers (*Talitrus saltator*) keep well away from the sea. Although they can swim quite well, they become very vulnerable once they are in the water. Hoppers are present on the upper shore right through the year, with lots of tiny young ones in the summer. The creatures burrow into the beach above the high water mark. They moult their skins on the weakest neaps and early spring tides in a regular cycle and they are most active over the top of the springs. Heavy weather and a flooding spring tide will drive them from their burrows to migrate in droves up the beach out of reach of the waves. This regular migration takes place only in the summer.

In places where cliffs, walls or other obstructions prevent their escape from the rising tide and breaking waves, many hoppers may be swept into the sea in rough weather and the bass will then eat them. Sandhoppers occur mainly on sandy beaches where the smaller bass are more likely to feed on them.

MAGGOTS

The maggots of the seaweed fly (*Coelopa frigida*) must be the smallest items of food normally eaten by decent-sized bass. The interesting point about this is that it *is* possible to use these tiny creatures as bait. To be strictly accurate, the best method is to bait a small hook (size 10–12) with the normal white maggots used by coarse anglers. The conditions and methods for using maggots are described in some detail in the book *Operation Sea Angler*. To recap briefly, the maggots are generated in piles of rotting weed cast up near the high water mark. Every bass angler should get used to kicking over heaps of old seaweed and inspecting them for the little white larvae. At high water spring tides the maggots wash out of the weed and drift on to the surface of the sea. In this situation they are devoured in great quantities by grey mullet. As in many other situations, where the mullet go the bass go too.

Bass feed both on maggots which are swirling about beneath the surface and on surface floaters. Light float tackle will take the former fish and fly tackle armed with a floating, polyethylene maggot-fly and a bunch of maggots will take the latter. It is rarely possible to select for bass in these circumstances, but, whereas the mullet often cruise along with their mouths exposed, the bass swirl and splash, going down between mouthfuls. Sometimes it is possible, by using a tube or streamer fly or a fish strip on a small hook in place of a fly, to select surface-feeding bass from the midst of mullet shoals. Large bass can be caught in this way and I have had numbers between 4 and 8lb. A double-figure fish on dry fly is a definite possibility for some jammy devil.

Perhaps the thing to learn from this is that bass preoccupied with tiny food items can be caught, and never forget that small hooks, fished on suitable gear, will effectively hold even large and powerful fish.

3
Natural Baits

The bigger the prawn, the bigger will be the fish.
W. J. Wallis, *Where to Fish*, 1953

AV As Mike has already explained, bass eat a variety of foods and a number of different natural baits are successfully used for bass fishing. For much of the time it seems that availability and tradition dictate where different baits are used, and there are local patterns that have an established history.

Probably the most widely used baits are lugworms, ragworms, crabs, pieces of fish, small whole fish, prawns, squid and cuttlefish flesh, razorfish and clams. There are other items that are less popular, but which can also be good baits – for example, maggots, cheese, bread, and sea slaters.

The commonest pattern is to use worms, razorfish, clam or fish strips over sand and crabs or larger fish baits over rocks. This generally makes good sense, since the bass are more likely to be searching for crabs or fish on rocky ground and for worms and molluscs over sand.

Everyone should experiment in his own locality, since, while it is safe to say that these baits are all good ones, bass do show definite local and seasonal preferences, and even different sizes of bass may choose different baits. When these preferences have been discovered, you can be confident that you are more likely to be using the right bait in the right place at the right time. One thing, however, is constant: to catch decent-sized bass regularly, then with few exceptions whatever bait you use should be a big one.

CRABS

Any angler who has not discovered what a marvellous bait soft or peeler crab is has not lived. In many situations crab is the number one natural shore-fishing bait for bass, particularly larger bass (and for several other species of fish). I well remember that I was nothing short of astonished when I found just how good a bait it is. Crab is the bait that has produced the majority of my medium-size and larger bass.

The crabs that are most useful to the angler are the common shore crab, the edible crab and the velvet fiddler crab. You are restricted in many places to whatever species you can find easily, and often the green or common shore crab is the only one readily available. All three types of crab make excellent baits, but in my experience edible crabs are better than shore crabs; limited use suggests that velvets are also superior. Other anglers confirm that in some areas velvets are, like edibles, better baits than shore crabs. Not only are edibles and velvets bigger, but there seems to be something extra that makes them more attractive. The difference in attractiveness is clear only on some shores. For example, two places where I have regularly caught good bass are only a couple of miles apart and in the one locality (Anglesey, between Beaumaris and Penmon) the fish take any crab equally well, whereas in the Menai Straits proper it is not really worth using shore crab, since the bass much prefer edibles. These conclusions have emerged over fifteen years of using both types of crab in both areas. Gut contents reflect the preference and, not surprisingly, the fish over the more rocky Menai Straits ground can find, and choose to eat, more edible crabs. Fish in the other locality are over mixed ground with a lot of rock, but bordering on sand flats, and their appetite is more catholic, there being more small flatfish and gurnards in the guts, as well as the different crabs.

Shore crabs can be found almost anywhere, but the best places to look for soft and peeler crabs are where there are rocks covered with wrack or kelp, particularly near the low water mark. The crabs can be found sheltering under the rocks and weed or in sand and mud around the edges of rocks. Along the stone walls of harbours, jetties and sea walls there is often a curtain of wrack at low water. If you walk along the base of the wall and lift the curtain many shore crabs can be found and dislodged from the joints between the stone blocks.

On some seemingly barren sandy shores, soft and peeler shore crabs can often be found in pools, even near high water mark.

Permanent streams tend to concentrate the crabs, which burrow into the sediment, and, if groynes are present, the pools of water they usually have at the bases of the uprights will frequently contain crabs. The crabs found will usually be on the small side, but early in the season the larger male peelers can provide the angler with good bait.

Soft crabs can be easily recognised by touch and are more frequently found in weed than peelers; peelers are less obvious. Crabs being held underneath other crabs are invariably female peelers, if they are the correct way up. If they are upside down they are soft, and the female beneath is mating with the cock crab above. So, if a pair are found together in this manner, the crab underneath is *always* worth taking and, conversely, the one above is never any use. This rule applies to all crabs (although it is much rarer to find pairs of edibles and velvets).

Hard crabs discovered alone must be tested to see if they are peelers. The end joint of a leg is twisted and removed to see whether there is a brightly coloured new skin underneath the old shell; if there is then the crab is a peeler (ready to moult or peel). If there is white connective tissue and muscle, then the crab is not

Baiting up with half of a large peeler edible crab. Note that the eye of the hook lies outside bait to prevent slumping on hook.

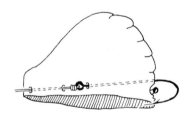

Large piece of edible crab

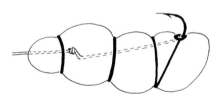

Elastic band secures crab

Baiting up with peeler or soft crab. A, B and C show how to secure crabs.

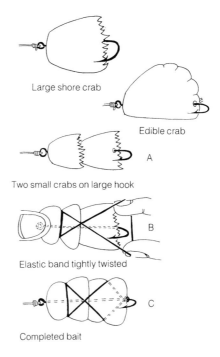

Large shore crab

Edible crab

A

Two small crabs on large hook

B

Elastic band tightly twisted

C

Completed bait

ready to peel and is no use to the bass angler (the crab will grow a new joint at its next moult).

Peeler crabs of both sexes are duller in colour and more likely to be covered in barnacles. Brightly coloured crabs are never peelers and, after a certain amount of experience, it becomes a matter of course to discard most hard crabs after a quick look. When the season is under way, most peelers can be recognised by appearance alone and the leg-joint test is just confirmation. It has been written more than once that peelers are not aggressive, but this is a misleading statement. Whilst a crab just about to shed its shell will be inactive, the majority of peelers are fierce and quite capable of giving you a sharp nip. When a crab actually peels, the shell cracks at the rear edge and around the sides first, so any crab showing these tell-tale cracks is a peeler, and must be used quickly, or else frozen, since it will not live if it tries to peel out of water.

Shore crabs (and any others) make attractive baits as peelers, soft crabs, or at any texture up to the crisp (hardening shell) stage. Most anglers discard crisp crabs, but be assured that they catch bass very effectively; if there are some parts that seem rather hard (for example, round the front edge) these parts can be removed.

A velvet swimmer in perfect peeling condition, showing the new shell under the old.

Big bass are far more likely to take a large crispy than a small softy.

Shore crabs are very easy to keep for days or even weeks. The softies do not harden up as quickly as many writers suggest, and, in any case, it doesn't really matter since they are still usable even if they go crisp. I keep crabs in plastic buckets and cover them with seaweed of the wrack type. Before leaving the beach the crabs are rinsed with sea water for a few minutes to wash and refresh them, then every drop of water is emptied out. It is important to remove all water, since crabs at the bottom will die if stagnant sea water is left there. It is best to keep softies separate, since they often become damaged by the hard-shelled and more active peelers.

The crabs are best given a dunk every day – or, rather, a rinse in sea water for five minutes or so. Treated in this way and kept in the cool, they will last for many days with the exception of moulting peelers, which must be taken out and frozen down or, alternatively, kept in the fridge to delay peeling. Peelers freeze very well, just as they are, and they are easier to peel on thawing. Frozen peelers also make excellent baits.

Crabs can be kept in tanks successfully, and if the water

temperature is about 5°C the peeling process is delayed. As crabs reach the cracking stage they can either be used in peak condition or frozen. Shore crabs and edibles can be kept easily enough, but velvets do not seem to survive in tanks. I have not tanked crabs myself, but have seen an excellent set-up in action. The angler concerned had overcome small practical problems in the system and used efficient cooling and filtering systems. He had a large amount of bait in superb condition ready for any occasion.

Baiting up is a matter for personal preference. However, one thing is certain: bass don't give a damn what their crab looks like and it is time wasted if you try to make your bait look like a crab. With shore crabs, legs of peelers can be left on or removed, it doesn't really matter, and no shore crab is big enough to be cut up into pieces for bass. Peelers are best if the body is more or less completely peeled, and crabs must then be securely fastened to the hook. Most anglers bind the crab with shirring elastic, but this tends eventually to clog up a hook and there is a temptation to use too much. I use small elastic bands which I carefully wash beforehand, working on the principle that if I can taste that bitterness of new elastic bands bass can as well, and it is best to

Two fish of 8½lb from the Menai Straits. One took a peeler edible crab, the other was hooked in shallow water on a very large 'doctored' edible on a two-hook rig.

43

Soft edible crab with its cast shell. Note the increase in size of the soft crab.

eliminate that possible disadvantage. Crabs must be firmly bound to the hook; I use a 5/0 which I open out a bit to make sure the point is where it can connect with the fish. The main considerations are that the bait should be big enough and that the point is not masked. I usually use two or three shore crabs at a time.

Edible crabs are found on more exposed shores than shore crabs, and do not venture so far up the beach. Edibles are more likely to be under rocks and rock ledges and, though sometimes they are rather less easy to find, they are bigger and better baits. It is rarer to find paired edible crabs, and potential peelers need to be tested. However, they are invariably darker-looking and often covered with barnacles. Edible crabs are slower-moving (out of water) than shore crabs, but have very powerful pincers (you have been warned). These crabs are protected by law below the size of 13cm across the carapace (back), but many of them are bigger than this, so in suitable territory there is little problem in finding crabs big enough. Many edibles are sufficiently large to be cut into two or more pieces for bait and a collection of peeled claws and legs can also make a superb bait.

A bonus feature of edible crabs is that, should one be found that really is too crisp to use, almost hard, it can be repeeled to reveal another new skin. The new shell can be taken off after careful cracking and the body part may be used as an ultra-soft softy. I have tended over the years to refer to these as 'doctored edibles' and when looking through my fishing diary, I see many instances of bass caught on them, including one fish of over 10lb. The only disadvantage to using doctored edibles is that the bait doesn't last so long and rebaiting needs to be more frequent. After ten minutes it is best to bait up again, whereas a normal bait can last up to twice as long.

Although moulting shore crabs and edible crabs can be found relatively easily from May to October, velvet fiddlers, on the shores that I know, are usually found in any quantity as softies or peelers only in late July, August and September. However, they seem to peel *en masse* and, if you are lucky enough to live near an exposed shore where velvets are common, you may find many in one go on the big spring tides at that time of year – an ideal opportunity to freeze some down for the last few weeks of the season, when bait is difficult to come by.

There are a few other points that may be of interest. Crabbing is

Jelly-soft edible crab – the right size for a good bass bait.

better on spring tides and best on tides that are increasing in range: the retreating crabs can then be followed down to the successively receding low water marks.

Edible crabs are more difficult to keep alive than shore crabs; they need rinsing with sea water at least daily and, despite their robust appearance, die rather easily. Peeler edibles often die overnight and, if they cannot be used within 24 hours, I freeze them straight away. Softies last longer, especially if they are kept in a fridge.

Velvet fiddlers may be dead even before you leave the beach, and rarely last a night out of water, so you need to use them immediately, or make other arrangements to avoid a bucket full of dead crabs. While I know of one 9½lb bass caught on a stinking crab, I have no faith in them myself.

For the angler with difficulties in collecting enough crabs for bait, an alternative strategy may be to set traps for shore crabs. On any expanse of sand or mud along a sheltered shore, for example in an estuary, various articles can be used to provide focal points for crabs. At the same time they tend to select for peelers and soft crabs. Probably the best traps are made from guttering and angled roof tiles. Sections of about two feet long are pushed into the sand or mud, or laid on it. Traps are best placed near the low water mark and both peelers and softies will be found to shelter under the trap, or in the angle where the trap enters the sediment. Traps can be extremely productive in season; often most traps will house useful crabs and collection is very easy. The only problem is that you need to make sure you are the first one to visit your traps.

Some anglers prefer to wear gloves to collect crabs, but when crabbing under water or feeling inside a crevice it is important to instantly feel and recognise the attitude of a crab so that it can immediately be grabbed, and this is impossible if gloves are worn. Take care to avoid too many cuts and scratches, although a few are unavoidable, almost obligatory. Take extra care in places where broken glass is likely to accumulate.

A ¼-inch steel rod about two feet long and turned round to make a small open curve at one end is useful for removing crabs from crevices or from beneath large rocks that cannot be turned. Some bait collectors use a smaller hook for turning weed and small rocks to avoid too much wear and tear on the skin.

It is to the advantage of the angler to leave rocks the right way

A two-fish catch from The Hole – bass of 11lb 4oz and 5lb 10oz.

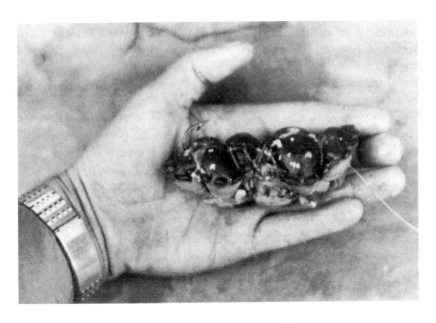

A good-sized peeler edible crab fastened to a 5/0 hook with elastic bands. Note the hook point standing well clear of the bait. (The gape of the hook has been widened by bending with pliers.)

up, since trapped seaweed rots and crabs then avoid it. Rocks left the wrong way up will also lead to the death of many other organisms, so please return rocks to the correct position when you are bait collecting.

Scientists at the University of Wales Institute of Science and Technology have studied crabbing grounds on the Mumbles Head foreshore, where, in popular areas, boulders were each turned over between forty and sixty times a year between May and September when the crabs were moulting. Even in less popular areas, the boulders were turned as many as ten times. Very few anglers (bait collectors) bothered to return the rocks to their former positions. It was concluded that as a result of this carelessness the death of weeds and animals had impoverished the shore life. It was thought that the crab stocks were replenished from below the low water mark but, since the attraction of a beach for fish lies in the whole of the life present, it has got to be good sense to return boulders as they originally were.

Finally, when using crab for bait, it is humane to kill them before baiting up. The crab's 'brain' is more or less in the centre on the underside of the body and the sharp point of a knife thrust in underneath should kill a crab instantly.

FISH BAITS

The fish baits most commonly used are sandeels and strips of mackerel (or herring) and these baits catch many different fish. However, when bass fishing, whilst one can never ignore sandeels or mackerel (particularly used as whole fillets or the head and guts), a wide variety of other small fish also make excellent baits, particularly for the bigger bass.

In different localities, on different beaches, anglers have their own preferences. In some areas small pouting are easily caught and take many bass. In other places blennies, butterfish or rocklings are used to good effect. These baits are seldom very much publicised since relatively few anglers persist with them, but local experts often make good catches on their own specialities.

My own initiation to the use of fish baits for bass was a result of talking with anglers on the Isle of Wight. In that locality, they rarely use crab, mainly for the simple reason that it 'just isn't done

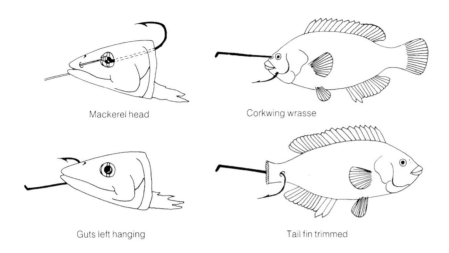

Mackerel head

Corkwing wrasse

Guts left hanging

Tail fin trimmed

Alternative ways of baiting with fish head or whole small dead fish. Tail-hooked wrasse (or other species) should have the tail fin trimmed off to prevent line twist.

here'. Sea anglers are remarkably conservative about baits and methods and the Isle of Wight (my own patch at that time) was no exception. The reason usually given was that crabs could not easily be collected, though after some exploration I found enough crabs for bait, and good bass catches resulted from their use. John Squibb, a friend and successful bass angler, first introduced me to the local speciality that he and several other anglers developed about thirty years ago. John's innovation was the use of small wrasse as bass baits. In turn he was shown how to use crabs. At the time it was a revelation to discover just how good wrasse are as bass baits in that area. The night when I caught three good bass on wrasse, including a nine-pounder, was an eye-opener.

Small whole fish usually have the property of being tougher than mackerel, and in that respect are better; they are also easier to obtain fresh. In a particular locality bass may indeed be searching for small rockling and wrasse, and my suggestion is not to automatically use sandeel or mackerel but to experiment with common local species. Catching nothing on rocklings for one or two sessions does not mean that bass would have been caught if

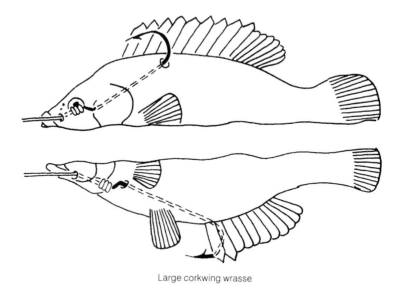

Large corkwing wrasse

A good method of cutting up larger wrasse to make suitable baits for big bass. Again, the fins may be trimmed to make a neater bait. The eye of the hook lies outside bait to prevent slumping.

mackerel had been the bait, just because 'a ten-pounder was caught there on mackerel last week'. It probably means that when you fished the bass weren't there. I have caught bass on a variety of fish baits, including a ten-pounder on mackerel, but I am still more confident when using a wrasse.

As in the case of crab, the detailed appearance of a dead fish bait presented on leger tackle matters little. A whole fish or a piece will catch bass, but the most attractive part seems to be the head and guts (this applies for conger as well).

As always, it is most important to leave plenty of hook point exposed and this can often conveniently be done if the bait is hung on the hook through the lips or root of the tail (in this case, the tail fin is cut off to avoid line twist and masking the hook point). I use a 5/0 hook and never worry about it showing; bass are not hook shy and it does not matter if the whole hook is visible. A 5/0 hook may seem large to someone who uses worm baits regularly, but

A 7³/4lb bass is played out and ready for the net.

any bass of two pounds or more will have no problem in engulfing it. Indeed, a 5/0 hook looks quite small in the mouth of a bass of 6lb or more.

I remember that when I was learning about using small fish for bass baits I had been told that 'down here [the Isle of Wight] you won't catch big bass on crab, and you won't catch small bass on wrasse'. That statement was fresh in my mind when I had a bite on a wrasse head followed by several feet of slack line. Imagine my surprise when I reeled in a portly little bass of 12oz with the large hook in its mouth. That was, however, quite easily the smallest bass I have caught on this bait and it is a fact that fish baits are particularly attractive to big bass.

Whilst on this subject, it is in order to mention livebaiting, even though some anglers find it distasteful. One of the commoner methods of bass fishing is probably using live sandeels, usually from a boat, when they can be extremely killing baits. The main problem with sandeels has always been keeping them alive. These days a bucket of sea water with a portable aerator can be used, but another method that works is to put the eels in a shallow box of wet sand. The eels burrow in and lie with their mouths at the surface; in this way they can be kept alive for several hours.

Any livebait is almost bound to be better than a deadbait as regards attractiveness, but there are a number of problems. It is sometimes difficult to obtain live fish baits and any attempt at casting a livebait may well kill it. However, it is possible to use various fish alive as baits and, since close-range fishing will often produce bass, the method is often quite practical from the shore. Livebaiting on rocky, weedy ground can be difficult if a long trace is used, since the bait may well take refuge in a very safe crack or clump of weed; the use of a paternoster for this type of fishing is recommended. A float could be used in many situations to keep the livebait from finding a haven, and the float needs to be just big enough to resist the attempts of the bait to drag it under.

Probably the ultimate in livebaiting for bass is a method used in South Wales by Lyndon Lammas. Mackerel are caught and then freelined as bait. To date, Lyndon has not had a ten-pounder this way, but eight-pounders are the rule with this method when it can be used. A similar approach has been developed to take bass

Various methods of hooking up livebaits for bass.

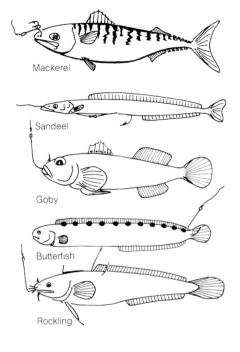

Mackerel

Sandeel

Goby

Butterfish

Rockling

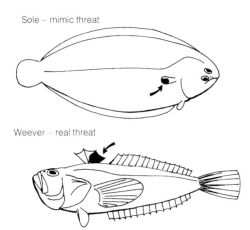

Sole – mimic threat

'Black-flag' threat of the poisonous lesser weever and the mimic threat of the Dover sole. Either may deter an 'experienced' bass from eating the flag waver.

Weever – real threat

commercially off Portland Bill. In several parts of the country, live pouting have also proved to be excellent bass baits.

A good general rule must be that if any small fish is abundant in the area where you are fishing, then it should be good bass bait. Are there likely to be any exceptions to this rule? Some fish may be distasteful or even poisonous to bass. The obvious example is the weever, which advertises its threat by raising a black, flag-like dorsal fin. Any fish which is conspicuously marked with patches of black could be trying to warn off predators. The pectoral fin of the Dover sole has a tiny black flag and is believed to be an imitation weever fin.

When attempting to catch bass that are feeding on a particular fish, the logical order of effectiveness of the baits should be:

1. An actual live fish (appearance, smell and movement all perfect).
2. A spun dead fish (appearance and smell perfect and movement nearly so).
3. An artificial of similar appearance (movement good, appearance also good).
4. A legered or floated dead fish (appearance and smell good, movement not so good).
5. A piece of fish legered (smell good).

However, my experience suggests that, even though the last two options appear to be the least natural, they can be extremely effective methods.

In writing about fish baits I have tried to broaden the picture rather than concentrate on the traditional strip of mackerel or sandeel. It is essential for a bass angler to experiment and learn from his experiences if he is to succeed; it is fatal to do what 'you and your mates have always done'.

RAGWORMS

Ragworms of any species are rather better bait than lugworms for general bass fishing. They are tougher and more active, and the movement of a large ragworm makes it an ideal float-fishing bait. Ragworms are usually a good deal messier to collect than lug. King rag often live amongst rocks mixed with sloppy mud near the low water mark of spring tides. Digging for them can be extremely hard work. First the holes and trails that the worms make must be found, then a strong, narrow spade or fork is the best tool for shifting rocks and mud to create a hole. Rock after rock must be hacked away to expose the worms, which are sometimes enormous (up to two feet long). Many anglers seem to feel this effort is well worth while and certainly large ragworms of this sort catch quite a few good bass from the shore every year, and many big bass are taken on ragworm from boats fishing off the Essex coast.

While a float-fished ragworm is best presented to leave plenty of tail hanging and moving attractively, a bottom-fished bait need have no particular appearance. It will be found by scent and the main consideration is – as always – that it should be large enough.

White ragworms are also excellent baits and worth a special mention. They are even more active than most 'red rag' and again they are particularly useful as a float-fished bait. In most places anglers find large specimens hard to come by; these bigger worms tend to occur near the low water mark of spring tides and make excellent baits.

There was a time when the only natural bait I used for bass was white ragworm. This was in the days when, as a teenager, the only bassing easily available to me was the fishing on various piers on the Isle of Wight. As with red ragworm, it is advisable when float-fishing or drifting this bait in mid-water to have an active tail

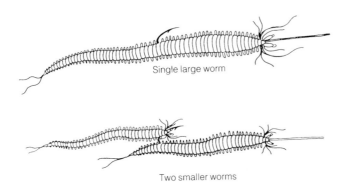

Single large worm

Two smaller worms

*When baiting up with ragworm to catch fish in mid-water it
pays to leave plenty of freely waving tail.*

Three four-pounders from Aber which took king rag baits.

on the hook or one worm on the hook and another dangling from it.

Incidentally, whereas a good way to keep lugworms or red ragworms in a satisfactory condition is on frequently changed newspaper, white rags are best kept in sand, covered with a little sea water; they quickly perish if they dry up. An old coffee jar is a suitable container.

LUGWORMS

Lugworms are quite easily dug and are widely used for fishing of a general nature. In the surf, where there are relatively few crabs to steal bait, they will take bass of all sizes; in Ireland they are almost universally used on the sandy strands. Lugworms make a streamlined, easy-to-cast hookful, and in many situations they are

Large lugworms, sometimes referred to as 'black lug' or 'sewie'.

a very sensible choice. Common lugworms must be threaded on to a hook and the trace above it, leaving little of the animal dangling, for they are relatively soft and will easily be torn off a hook. However, over any bottom where there are many crabs and small fish to steal baits, lugworms are less useful as a specialist bass bait. As with all worm baits, they are likely to be taken by any fish, large or small, and particularly by small bass.

The familiar lugworm (*Arenicola marina*), with a swollen front end and thinner tail, seems to behave as if there are two distinct varieties. The commoner 'blow lug' is smaller, up to about seven inches long, and lives in a U-shaped burrow between the tidelines, mainly on more sheltered sandy shores. They can be easily dug, since they are not often deeper than about twelve inches, and they occur in the middle levels of the shore, so they are usually available even on neap tides. Where many are found together, they can be dug by trenching with a fork. Where fewer worms are found, they are better dug up singly. The blow-hole is paired with its cast and a small spit removed with a spade before the second, deeper, cut removes the worm.

The other variety, black lug, is larger, usually darker in colour, much tougher and found only towards extreme low water marks. These worms burrow straight down and are found lying vertically, up to two feet or more deep. There is no separate blow-hole and the cast is a much neater coil than the squiggly pile of the smaller blow lug. A small spade with a straight, narrow blade is the best tool to use and the sand is removed to follow the worm's burrow until either the tail is exposed or no more sand can be removed. Then, bare-armed, you plunge your hand down and feel about in the sloppy sand for the head end of the worm, which you grip firmly, to pull up the animal. This is quite a tricky business and practice is required.

The larger black lug tend to blow out their own guts, which are messy, and unless the worms are to be used straight away it is best for the angler to squeeze out the gut as each worm is dug up. Black lug are best kept wrapped in newspaper in the fridge, where they will last for several days and still appear to be alive.

These days a number of anglers successfully keep worms in cooled, aerated tanks, and if you have a suitable tank which you can rig with a filter it is worth using this method. At 5°C ragworms or lugworms will remain in good condition for several weeks.

However, Mike and I have not tried this ourselves and rarely does either of us use worms for bass bait nowadays.

SQUID AND CUTTLEFISH

These close relatives are commoner than most anglers realise, and large pieces of them make excellent baits; small whole squid can also be used. As with all bottom-fished baits, the appearance is not as important as having the hook point exposed. This fact needs to be stressed, more so with squid and cuttle than with most other baits, since the flesh is very pliable and also extremely tough. This toughness is an advantage because a bait lasts a long time, but the disadvantage is that the hook will not pull through the flesh on the strike. Most anglers must, at some time, have failed to hook fish because the point became embedded in a piece of the bait which had flopped over it. For that reason, it pays to thread a strip of squid on to the hook and have the point near the bottom end, so that the bait cannot mask the point. Cuttlefish and big squid are better in this respect, since they have thicker and therefore stiffer flesh. If small squid are used, they may need to be tied with shirring elastic or rubber bands to prevent them slumping on the hook bend. Turned-down eyes on hooks also help to support the flesh. A two-hook tackle is also useful when baiting with squid.

I have caught bass on squid and cuttlefish baits even when they have been in the water for half an hour or more. They are so tough (in the larger specimens) that the crabs take ages to demolish them, and they still seem to be attractive after a long dunking. This bait

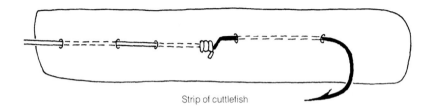

Strip of cuttlefish

When baiting with cuttle or squid, thread the bait so that the eye of the hook prevents the bait slumping down.

tends to select bigger bass, and occasionally fish become preoccupied with it.

To illustrate this point, I recall one trip when I found myself fishing about fifteen yards away from another bass angler on a rocky ledge on the Isle of Wight. It was dark and I was using my favourite bait, wrasse; I knew that the other angler also used wrasse a lot and was expecting him to be using more or less identical tackle and bait. However, I had a very frustrating time, since after an hour and a half I had only one bite and my companion had many bites (judging from the many strikes he made) and he landed two fine bass of 5 or 6lb, together with a conger of about 10lb. Wandering across to see what might be learned from the situation, I discovered that he was using cuttle. Obviously, the fish were interested in cuttle and, quite likely, nothing much else on that occasion.

Brian Warne, an experienced Isle of Wight angler, has told me that every year there is a time, early in the season, when the bass have this preoccupation with cuttlefish. Usually it will be the better fish that respond to this bait.

Mike, like myself, has found that squid or cuttlefish is often a good bait in rough autumn weather. On one occasion the sea was filthy when he and his friend Jon Bass arrived at Chapman's Pool, Dorset, after a September storm. Even though they spent some time spinning with large plugs, the fish showed no interest. The bass were definitely present since several had shown on the surface ten or fifteen yards out. They had brought half a dozen calamari squid and, deciding that the fish might prefer a natural bait, Jon had fixed up a simple float rig with a whole squid suspended eighteen inches below the surface. As they watched the little cork bobbing about on the choppy, murky surface, a fine fish rolled like a porpoise five or six yards beyond it. They waited hopefully for ten seconds, twenty, thirty – the cork was still there and they began to relax. Clearly their optimism had been misplaced. After all, why should the fish take the squid? Just as their nerves settled down, the cork whipped away and a convulsive strike set the hook into a fine bass. The fish fought well and when it was landed it scaled 8½lb. It seemed that the bass had taken the best part of a minute to find a big squid bait at a distance which it could have covered in two or three seconds. Perhaps this is an indication of the value of a large, smelly squid bait in coloured water.

RAZORFISH AND CLAMS

These baits are normally used over sand, particularly in the context of surf fishing, and both are excellent. Razorfish are only locally distributed between the tide marks, and the bigger variety is found only on the lowest springs.

The way to find razors is to look for the distinctive neat oval hole. This hole becomes a much larger muddy depression if the animal is disturbed, and this is why bait collectors walk backwards over the sand looking for the hole or tell-tale muddy squirt of water.

Razorfish can be speared (this takes practice) or they can be brought up to the surface by placing salt on top of the hole, which seems to irritate the animal, for it then comes up, often leaving the burrow completely.

In some places razors (especially the smaller ones) can be dug up with a fork. It is also possible to catch them by hand when the sand is still covered by water on the ebb. The hole is located and two fingers are gently slid either side of the hole about two inches deep. The razor is usually right at the top of its burrow and the shell can be held with the two fingers until the other hand gets a firm enough grip to pull it out. This method requires clear, calm water and knowledge of a razor bed, as the angler follows the ebbing tide back.

Clams can easily be dug because they live in stiff muddy sand, leaving a very neat oval hole. As with razors, they are very locally distributed and may not be available to many anglers, but they often occur well up the shore, in estuaries and on other sheltered beaches.

To use razorfish as bait, the whole foot is threaded up the line with the hook near the end. A large razor makes a handsome and attractive bait for bass of all sizes. Fresh razor is tough and stays in position well, but frozen razor becomes very soft and needs to be tied on securely. Clams are also used whole; the brownish siphon is very tough, but the softer body may need to be tied on.

Both razorfish and clams last quite well out of water if they are kept cool, although they may have to be frozen if a lot are collected together. Harry Parham of the Bass Anglers' Sportfishing Society (BASS) has great faith in clam as a bass bait and uses them, either fresh or frozen, from the beach at Paignton. Alan Yates has reported that if razorfish is parboiled (blanched) before freezing then it retains its toughness, but I have not tried this myself.

SLIPPER LIMPETS *('Knucklefish')*

These molluscs are not native animals, and since they were accidentally introduced into Southampton Water they have spread along the south of England up to South Wales. They are not a premier bait for bass but when they are washed up after a blow they are easily collected, and half a dozen or so presented on a hook make a useful bait. Certainly bass will take them. Brian Warne has found that they are a much better bait when really high, and prefers to keep them for a week or so until they stink.

PRAWNS AND SHRIMPS

Several species of prawns and their relatives the shrimps can be used for bass. Prawns are commonly found near rocks, amongst weed and in pools, or around pier piles, whereas shrimps are found in and over sandy bottoms. Prawns are generally a better

Fish of many sorts, including bass, concentrate near the piles under a pier.

A live prawn bait – excellent for float fishing where wrasse are not a problem.

proposition for the angler since they tend to be bigger than shrimps and are easily caught with a small net, especially in the shady areas of pools under seaweed, or by using a baited drop net in deeper water. They survive quite well if covered with damp seaweed. Mike and I have had limited success when using prawns, but shrimps are really an unknown quantity as far as we are concerned; they are probably on a par with prawns.

Prawns are a visual bait. They are best fished live beneath a float or drift-lined from some vantage point. They should be hooked through the back end of the abdomen and will survive for quite a time on the hook, which, according to the size of the prawn, should be about size 2–2/0, short-shanked and fine wire. Prawns are most frequently used, and are most effective, in summer where there is clear water and the bass are probably finding food easy to come by. The kind of conditions less favourable for legering with crab, fish or worms (calm, clear water) are not the kiss of death for fishing with prawns. Prawns can be a killing bait, taking excellent catches, often of big fish, for anglers expert in their use. When I have used prawns, I have caught only small fish, but this is perhaps a reflection on the locality and the limited amount of time I put in.

Incidentally, Clive Gammon once wrote to me that his biggest bass, a twelve-pounder, was caught on a small single live prawn.

In years past prawns were considered to be a premier bait for bass and were certainly widely used. In the Portland area of Dorset they were regarded as a necessity, and there was also a tradition of using 'red prawns' at Barry in South Wales. In 1921 F. D. Holcombe placed prawns about on a par with sandeels as bass baits. A short-shanked hook and little or no lead was the standard method and dead prawns were said to be 'nearly useless'. Clearly the jerky movements of the crustacean were recognised as the main attraction to the bass.

F. B. Hannam, writing of fishing at Osmington Mills near Weymouth in 1922, gives the following account of bass taken in shallow water with an unleaded float and live prawns: ' . . . he had three nice fish of 4, 5 and 6lb . . . Next day they [two of them] had five fish weighing 25lb . . . they went four times, catching four, five or six fish each day, but the last day they tried there it was a blank.' He recalls that the fish were swimming, at high water, in shallow water, practically on the beach. One 6lb fish was taken only six inches below the float.

Hannam also reports a catch of ten fish weighing 50lb taken on prawn in the space of half an hour, and a fish of 12lb taken by Mr Summers (a well-known local bass angler) on the same bait.

Mike makes the valid point that prawns tend to be very attractive to wrasse and small pollack in some areas where bass would be expected. However, he has also had the experience of finding that bass will take prawns when other baits and lures have failed to induce a bite. He has reported elsewhere that dusk and dawn and the ebbing spring tide are periods of particular activity for prawns. This fits in with the observations of prawn-fishing experts as to the best times to use this bait.

SMALL NATURAL BAITS

Maggots, sea slaters and sandhoppers are all valuable bass baits. It is proven fact that bass do feed heavily on these items under conditions where they are available in quantity, and a carefully presented natural or artificial bait, using light tackle either fly-fished, drifted or floated, is quite likely to take fish.

OTHER BAITS

Occasionally bass are caught on baits which are very unusual in the bass-fishing context. I know of quite a few taken on bread by mullet anglers fishing from the piers of the Isle of Wight. In 1975 Philip Smith took an 11lb bass on bread paste, using 4½lb line, from Nell's Point at Barry, and in the same year Ronald Davies beat a 16lb bass from Friar's Point in Barry using 6lb line and bread paste.

Aber on the late flood.

Less conventionally, bass have been caught on cheese baits. Again, an example will make the point. John Squibb from the Isle of Wight regularly ate his packed lunch, with a number of workmates, by the River Medina at Cowes. The remains of sandwiches would, inevitably, be thrown into the river and John noticed that bass were mopping up the bits of sandwich. Always keen to experiment, John tried float fishing during his dinner hour, with cheddar cheese on the hook. He caught several bass on this unusual bait and the biggest, a six-pounder, had its stomach crammed with cheese!

4
Tackling Up for Bass

The most suitable weapon to use is a light spinning rod, about 10ft or 11ft in length.

F. D. Holcombe, *Modern Sea Angling*, 1921

Fishing tackle is a very personal thing. A broomshank, Scarborough reel and flax line in the hands of an angler of many years experience will surely catch more and bigger fish than the latest boron wand, £100+ multiplier and ultra-strong nylon used by a novice with no idea of where, when or how to fish. In this chapter we describe the gear which experience has shown to be effective for our own styles of fishing and on the shores with which we are familiar.

LEGERING AND FLOAT FISHING

AV Bass have a reputation for hard biting and strong pulling; certainly they are strong and game fish, but only under certain circumstances do they take bait in a reckless fashion. They do this when they need to grab it there and then or risk losing it altogether. Typically this happens when they are taking small fish, for example when they are feeding voraciously on a shoal of sandeels. Indeed, my experience suggests that bass generally take a lure in a very positive manner with the result that they often hook themselves.

Bass also bite freely when they are feeding in the surf. Under these circumstances, any item of food is probably on the move and must be seized in a hurry. When the fish in a shoal are feeding together there is likely to be hot competition for food and a bass would risk going hungry if it was slow to take its chance of a meal.

In rough weather, crabs and small fish will be washed out of rocks and helplessly swirled around and this can often be exploited when fishing on exposed shorelines. On sheltered shores the heavy weed growth lashing around in the waves and the amount of loose drifting weed fragments usually makes fishing difficult. Bass are always opportunist feeders and, being strong swimmers, they will come right into the shallows, even in heavy sea conditions over rocks, to mop up items of food exposed by the storm. This partly explains the frequently quoted association between good bass fishing and rough seas.

However, even in conditions such as these, bass can be quick to reject a bait with strings attached, so the rod must be held and an immediate strike made in response to violent bites. Again, this fits in well with the traditional advice. The speed with which bass reject a bait if they feel unexpected resistance is perhaps the main reason why many anglers do not catch numbers of good bass.

Under conditions of less urgency, larger bass take a bait very gently and virtually never attempt to swallow it in a hurry. Despite this wary attitude, bass can be caught in calm conditions when they have ample time to inspect and choose their food. In these circumstances they will rarely hook themselves and the rod left in a rest to fish for itself may not even register a bite, though a bass has sampled the bait, felt the resisting lead and departed.

It follows from all this that the gear used, the arrangement of terminal tackle and the way that the angler reacts to a take are critical. Everything must be geared to not alarming the fish. The lightest lead – or no lead at all – should be used and a running line is always better than a fixed paternoster if the fish are cautious. Bass feed very close in, so it is not often necessary to cast very far – thirty yards is usually more than enough. A heavy casting weight is rarely required, so the whole outfit can be fairly light. This is an advantage because the rod needs to be held for long periods if the take of a fish is to be felt. Takes can be the gentlest of plucks (like a blenny moving the bait) and should be given slack line at once to allow the fish a chance to grasp the baited hook properly and get it well into the mouth.

When a bass has picked up a bait it then moves off. If the fish swims away from him, the angler feels a tightening of the line; often this is gentle and steady. Such bites should be taken as the signal to strike very hard. The mouth of a bass is very bony for the most part and nothing short of 'trying to pull its head off' will reliably set a big hook. Equally often the angler feels nothing at all,

A four-pounder neatly hooked in the corner of the mouth.

but suddenly realises that he has slack line; the fish has moved towards him and the amount of slack can be anything from a few inches to several yards. The temptation is to reel like mad and strike violently, but resist the temptation. The fish is coming towards you and a strike is likely to pull the bait out of its mouth. Also bass have good eyesight and if a large section of the horizon suddenly moves quickly, the fish may reject the bait and depart before you have time to make contact. The thing to do with a short-range, slack-line bite is to take up the slack ever so carefully, but on no account tighten completely on the fish. Usually a bumping sensation will be detected or a twitching will be felt down the line, but wait for a steady pull before striking. Such a pull means that the fish is now moving away and a strike will probably set the hook into the side of the mouth. Quite often several lots of slack line will have to be taken up before there is an opportunity for an effective strike. Each time this happens I have a minor heart attack, knowing that a bass has taken my bait and is very close, perhaps even close enough to see me, and I *must* do the right thing if I am to connect.

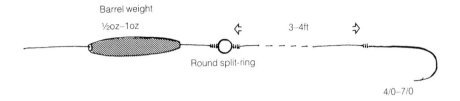

Simple running leger – effective over flat rock ledges or dense beds of kelp.

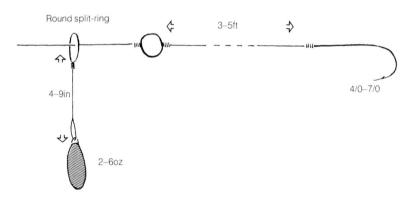

Running end-tackle for fishing over snaggy ground. A slightly rotten bottom is used for the weight link.

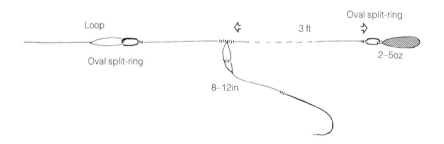

Fixed paternoster for tangle-free long-range fishing on surf beaches.

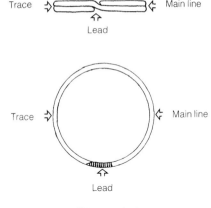

Method of using split-rings as links and/or stops for making up tackles.

Tying to split-ring

The possibility of the angler being seen by the bass might suggest that fishing in the hours of darkness would be more rewarding, but most of my bass have been caught in broad daylight. Much more important than day or night is what the tide is doing. Bass move in over rocks to a timetable of their own according to the state of the tide. It is up to the angler to discover this timetable for a particular venue, since, under similar conditions, the bass will stick to it by day and by night.

It should now be obvious that the clumsy or careless angler, splashing about or walking around, will frighten these fish which feed so close in to the shoreline in daytime. In this respect clumsy anglers *are* better off at night, but you don't have to fish in the hours of darkness to catch good bass consistently. Only one of my double-figure fish was caught after dark and Mike confirms that the great majority of the bass which he catches are taken in the hours of daylight.

So what of the commonly held belief that surf bassing is not so good in daylight, even on storm beaches? Perhaps in some situations, where there may even be a lot of human activity on the shore in daytime, the lack of cover is important. It may well be that during daylight bass prefer to keep to the places where rocks and weed provide cover. This was certainly the pattern at a venue which I once fished regularly on a very sheltered stretch of shore. The bottom was muddy sand, very flat and shallow, close to an estuary mouth. The fish arrived at high water, but only at night. It seems to me that on open sandy or muddy beaches the fishing usually improves after dark. Over rocky ground, in contrast, where the fish will usually be bigger, daylight fishing pays off handsomely.

Where does this get us regarding tackle? First of all, consider legering. When fishing at distance in the surf, where bass take well and where fish and angler feel the resistance of each other simultaneously, the form of terminal tackle is not too critical. However, most expert surf-bass men like a good length between the lead and the hook; it seems that having a bait and lead too close together puts a fish off. The movement of the surf can tie a long trace into a ball of knitting, so the sensible choice is either a fixed or running paternoster with the lightest lead usable. A light breakaway lead is better than a heavy wired one; a light lead with no wires is better still. A small pyramid with flat sides will hold better than a larger bomb and, because it is less inclined to roll, will cause fewer tangles.

For fishing closer, and in situations where bass are going to take

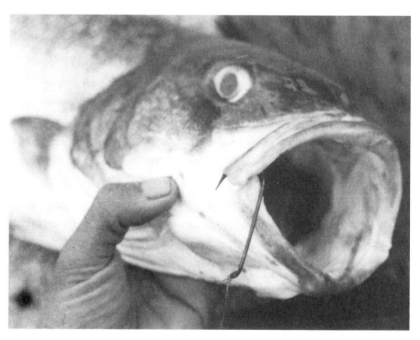

A 5/0 hook does not seem large in the mouth of a 6lb bass.

more time over selecting their food, a running lead is a must. Again the lightest possible weight must be used and, in my experience, a long trace can make the difference between big fish and nothing at all. A long trace gives less chance of a taking fish coming hard up against the resistance of the rest of the tackle. Surprisingly, the thickness of the line is not usually all that critical. The best compromise is to use the lightest line that gives a reasonable chance of retrieving the tackle without too many losses. It's crazy to use 10lb mono through to the hook if you are bottom fishing over barnacle-covered craggy rocks, yet it might be possible to go that light in sandy areas. In most conditions the fish are certainly not put off by lines of from 15 to 20lb breaking strain. Over rocks I use from 15 to 30lb BS depending on just how rough the bottom is. In calm, clear, very shallow water I have found legering less successful (but in Chapter 7 Mike describes his success when using finer line at close range).

As to hooks, each angler should decide on the pattern which he prefers, and then hone every hook to a needle point (resharpening is necessary during the fishing session). I use a carborundum slip of stone 3 inches by 1 inch, which is available from hardware shops, and is cheaper than the ones marketed by tackle firms. Mike uses the same type, but breaks his with a hammer to produce several small sharpeners.

Baits should be large and most anglers will use a correspondingly large hook (I usually use a 4/0 or 5/0). My only real hobby-horse on this subject is that I can't abide the popular beaked 'bait-holder' hooks (neither can Mike); the theory of greater hooking power in these hooks is based on a straight pull into a surface at right angles to the point, and this situation is unlikely to occur in practical bass fishing. Also they are brittle, the barbs tear fingers and do not hold the bait effectively. I use bronzed hooks of the Viking pattern (Mustad 79510 or 79515) in size 4/0 or pattern 7780C in size 5/0. With both types of hook I bend out the point a bit to widen the gape; I am sure that this improves hooking power when using a large, bulky bait. I do not know whether silvered or gold-coloured hooks could put fish off, nor whether coloured elastic bands or shirring elastic used to secure baits could do the same. It seems sensible to match hook colour to bait colour where possible, and certainly it cannot do any harm. It would be interesting to hear from anyone who has evidence about the effect of hook colour on bite frequency.

In recent years a number of good hooks suitable for bass fishing have been marketed. These hooks tend to be relatively fine-wired, small in the barb and sharper than most. However, a few of the recent products are brittle, while some bend out under pressure, and these are best avoided.

I have no recommendations about the swivels or links at present available, other than the obvious one that they must be stronger than the line. In most cases swivels do not function under strain and therefore only operate as stops on the line. For this reason, for many years I opted to use round split-rings as a cheap alternative, particularly since for much of the time I am fishing where I can expect some tackle losses. There have been no problems with split-rings breaking, opening out or cutting the line in all that time, but I am careful to use good-quality rings and to tie knots well away from the sharp metal ends. Also, split-rings run on the line far better than most swivels and always give a freely running leger. The drawings show how I tackle up. These tackles work well and are based on what I consider to be sound theory.

Something else which must be stressed is that the tackles described are designed to catch fish as efficiently as possible, but they never become treasured collector's items. Terminal tackle is expendable and you must be prepared to lose end gear frequently at times if you are seeking out good bass. Much of the best fishing is in very snaggy areas. In this context it is vital to develop the ability to set up again quickly after losing tackle. Often the fish will be present only for a short time and speed is of the essence; a bait must be out there all the time.

It may be of interest if I mention how I first developed my methods of legering for bass. As a student I caught quite a lot of goodish bass, using a range of baits presented on standard beach fishing tackle, using running legers. I often fished in quite deep water in the Menai Straits and on some Welsh storm beaches, as well as in the relatively shallow waters of estuaries. When I left college and moved to the Isle of Wight, I discovered that the bass, which were obviously feeding in calm seas along the shallow, weedy shoreline, were virtually uncatchable on my standard 4oz running-leger tackle. I experimented with short casts and long casts, but only managed to contact one or two fish, which gave hurried pulls to announce their presence before they departed. The amount of lead was reduced to 3oz and I fished closer in to enable the tackle to hold bottom; the result was a single small bass. I reduced the weight still further and found it impossible to hold in the strong cross-current, but I caught two more bass. Finally, it became clear that by using only ¾ or 1oz on 15lb BS line and casting a mere twenty to twenty-five yards, I could regularly catch bass with little difficulty. In amongst the kelp, the lead that snagged least was a barrel, threaded directly on the main line.

In even stronger currents, or in deeper water, bass usually take a bait more confidently and in such situations a heavier lead can be used if necessary. However, in the event of a bite under these circumstances, slack line must be given instantly. Leads of up to 6oz may be necessary in extreme conditions, but this business is much less pleasurable, unless the venue is known to hold really big fish.

For about ten years I have used an Abu 403 9-foot hollow-glass spinning rod with a Mitchell fixed-spool reel, although I found the sliding reel-seat rather too ready to slide and substituted a lightweight Fuji fitting. This rod is a joy to use for close-range legering (as well as spinning and float fishing), but is not long enough or stiff enough to set a big hook at any distance. When I am casting more than thirty yards, I usually use an 11-foot carbon spinning rod with a fixed-spool reel or a light home-made beach rod and small multiplier.

The ideal line strength varies, but should, I repeat, be as light as is sensible and of a reliable brand (I use Sylcast or Damyl and find them all right).

I land my fish with a net, which must be large enough to cope with a big fish (mine is triangular with 30-inch arms). I would hate to find myself connected to a huge bass with no means of landing it. The problem could be acute in many rocky places.

Of course, another method of presenting a bait in such a way as to appear natural to a fish searching for food, and to give relatively little resistance to a taking bass, is to use balanced float tackle. Float fishing can most conveniently be carried out from piers or from a suitable rocky vantage point, but may also be used from the beach or over shallow reefs or banks. It is important to use the smallest float that will, first, support enough weight to cast the tackle to the required distance; second, support the weight of the

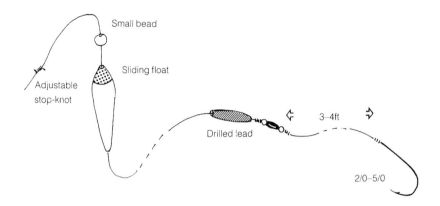

Sliding float tackle suitable for searching mixed ground and varied depths for bass.

bait and hook; third, be clearly visible when properly cocked; and, finally, be sufficiently buoyant to ride the swell or chop. A fixed float may be suitable in shallow water, but a sliding float is just as easy to rig and makes it easy to fish at any depth or distance. Suitable leads include barrels, balls, Wye leads, spirals and split shot. Even in moderately rough conditions, half an ounce is generally sufficient.

Usually float fishing for bass means close range and shallow water – from 3 to 6 feet. A bass taking the bait in these conditions will almost always take the float under or move it smartly sideways with a minimum of dithering. Fishing close in does, of course, mean that you must be particularly careful not to scare fish by splashing or moving about. Float fishing is a most pleasing way of catching bass and an opportunity for the angler to fish lighter than may be possible with other tactics. This, in turn, means that the fish are not likely to be scared by tackle resistance, unless the float is too big. Any of the baits mentioned in Chapter 3 can be used and one of the advantages of this type of fishing is that livebaits may be fished with ease. Probably the most successful baits under a float are crab, prawn, small fish and ragworm.

As always, the important thing is to think about how the bass are feeding and how you can maximise the chance of your tackle catching fish. Finesse is required, for, while bass sometimes take a bait fiercely, much of the best fishing is in shallow water, close to the shoreline, where fish may take their time. Only a delicate touch will bring success in these conditions; often you can be amazed at fish caught almost under your feet.

SPINNING

ML   The factors which govern the selection of tackle for spinning for bass are rather different from those affecting the choice of bottom-fishing gear. The fish are, of course, the same size – somewhere between a chub and a decent pike in weight – so, from the point of view of playing and landing the fish, rods of from 1fi to 2lb test curve are quite suitable (the old Abu legerlites were good examples). Since you are likely to be holding the rod for long periods and doing a lot of casting, there is no point using anything heavier than necessary. My own choice is a carp rod of from 10 to 12 feet in length. These rods are light to handle; they are also designed to cast light baits and many of the smaller bass lures weigh only a fraction of an ounce. The length of the rod allows the angler a high degree of control over the path and movements of the lure when it becomes necessary to manoeuvre in between rocks or weed clumps close in to the shore. Rods designed for carp fishing have plenty of backbone for setting decent-sized hooks into the leathery mouths of big fish; they are quite suitable for pulling a well sharpened point of a single or treble into the tough jaw of a lunging bass. The current fashion seems to be for carp and pike rods with test curves of $2\frac{1}{2}$–3lb – a bit on the powerful side for most bass spinning activities. I would still go for the something around the 2lb mark.

It is, of course, possible to obtain spinning rods made for the job and in the right sort of casting-weight range. The best of these are very good bass catchers and, for anyone who prefers a shorter rod (they are mostly 7–9 feet in length), they may be ideal. These rods can be obtained with actions ranging from all-through to tip-action; and any and all of them will work – that is to say that in experienced hands they will catch plenty of decent bass. My only grouse about spinning rods is that many of them have fixed positions for the reel fitting, which may or may not be either sensible or comfortable. On the other hand, the simple sliding reel seat of most carp rods is liable to slip in use and allow the reel to fall off, unless it is bound on with a half-inch strip of cycle inner-tube. Modern rods all tend to have good screw reel fittings and the problem of attaching reels no longer exists.

Much more important than the rod is the reel. Although a good multiplier is a reasonable choice for heavier lures, for fishing with light lures, often in rough, windy conditions, there is little point in considering anything but a fixed-spool reel. Most fixed-spools have an adequate line capacity for spinning, but the things to consider when making a choice are as follows, in order of importance.

A smooth, reliable clutch which can be adjusted to a wide range of tensions is my main criterion for a good reel. In spinning, the first requirement is to have a clutch setting such that a pull which is only a little less than the breaking strain of the line will just start the spool turning. This allows the angler to set the hook firmly in the mouth of a taking fish. One characteristic which is common to all clutches and may often be a disadvantage, but which is ideal for spinning, is the fact that it takes a good deal stronger pull to start the clutch moving than to keep it going. Because of this, you may not need to readjust the clutch while you are playing a fish. If it is necessary to ease off on a particularly large or fast-moving bass, then a rear drag adjustment is a useful feature.

A spool of decent diameter – say, 2½ inches – will assist smooth casting, as will a hard, smooth lip to the spool. Even more important is an effective level-wind mechanism, with no tendency to pile the line unevenly. Most good quality reels will have these characteristics, together with an effective and reliable bale-arm mechanism, a smooth, comparatively silent, train of gears and a positive anti-reverse.

Try to avoid reels with metal parts which will corrode in contact with sea water, because it is inevitable that the reel will be splashed, coated in spray or, on occasion, dropped into the drink. Brass, nylon and stainless steel are the right materials for the moving parts of bass spinning reels. If aluminium alloys are used (and most, if not all, reels have casings of this type) then they should be heavily anodised. Even the best-quality, 'salt-water-proof' reels will corrode if the coating is chipped or damaged in use. Liberal use of the oil can and, if you are a meticulous angler, rinsing in clean, warm water after a trip will keep this vital item of equipment in good nick.

The one thing *never* to do is to leave a wet or damp reel for any length of time in a poorly ventilated place (bag, box, car boot, etc.); nothing will ruin a reel more quickly.

For spinning with light lures a well filled spool is even more important than in most other forms of angling. Similarly, the line itself must be supple and have good knot strength. Never buy poor quality line for spinning because with big fish coming to the lure frequently in rough conditions there is no time for tangles and no margin for error. Sylcast is pretty good and it is very hard-wearing. Several other makes of line are also quite suitable. The various brands labelled as Kroic tend to be very fine spinning lines, if somewhat expensive, and I must confess to a personal preference for them. Maxima is widely used by many competent anglers. Ultimately, the reliability of a line depends on the angler himself and in no form of angling is this truer than in spinning for bass, because the lines are quite light and conditions can be very harsh. Lines of 8–10lb BS are quite suitable.

The golden rules are, first, renew the line at least at the start of every season, or if it is damaged in any way, or if it is low on the spool due to losses. Second, make sure that every knot is sound by tying it tidily and giving it a good pull to test the strength. If in doubt, tie it again. Third, when setting up, check the last couple of feet of line; check it again after any snag or fish, notably after catching or losing a wrasse, as well as after clearing the lure from hang-ups on ledges or boulders. You may get away with it time after time but, be assured, if you do not check, the occasion will arise when you hook a big bass, perhaps the only one of the day, only to feel that sickeningly sudden release of tension which means that you have lost both fish and lure. In all angling this is probably the saddest and emptiest emotion that you can experience.

Swivels and split-rings are generally of more than adequate strength, even in the smallest sizes. My own preference is for a very simple, small, spring-link swivel between line and lure, but any little, lightweight, reliable link will do. Try to avoid the sort of clip which will kink or angle itself in any way. A kinked link will kill the action of almost any lure and, when this occurs on every other cast, the frustration can be unbearable. Perhaps the best arrangement of all is the combination of a small swivel with a circular split-ring, which ensures that the lure is always mounted straight through from the line. Very strong split-rings can be difficult to open when your hands are cold, but a pair of artery forceps make a useful 'third hand' when lure changing. It is possible to tie fancy loops which avoid the need for metal links, but each knot or loop tied is a potential source of weakness.

For attaching spinning lures I now use the smallest size (16) of crosslock link (you can take the swivel off unless you intend using revolving lures). These seem very reliable and with a breaking strain in excess of 20lb are more than strong enough for the biggest bass. If these are difficult to get hold of, then the next size up (14) is okay, but try not to go any heavier. I still see anglers attaching light plugs with link swivels that would cope with bluefin tuna.

The only other item of spinning tackle to consider is the hook. Whether it is a single or a treble, it must be needle sharp, small in the barb and as fine in the wire as possible. It must also have sufficient strength to hold a big fish in a prolonged battle. Most good-quality hooks, of the sizes used, have ample strength to play and land any bass that swims. Never use hooks which show any inclination to snap under strain. It is always preferable for a hook to straighten gradually under tension. I like Au Lion d'Or 3005 or Eagle Claw trebles on my plugs and spoons, but, whatever type you choose, it is necessary to keep a constant eye open for points turned or blunted during fishing. (I still use Eagle Claw hooks.) Never cast out with a blunt hook, it really is not worth the risk of a missed fish. If you change the hooks on a lure for finer or lighter hooks, it may be necessary to add lead wire to the shanks to maintain the action of the lure. Alternatively, increase the hook size a little.

What about weights and anti-kinks? Essentially, very little lead or other weight is usually required for bass spinning. If it is at all possible, try to avoid adding lead to the line because it interferes with casting and complicates fishing. To achieve longer casts, if necessary, try to use more compact or denser lures. Even a small Toby will cast a long way on 8lb line. You can add lead to the lure itself, and a barrel lead inside a Redgill is very effective, whatever you may have read elsewhere. I cannot remember when I last spun for bass with any sort of up-trace weight.

What is the best lure for bass spinning? Just as in any other form of fishing, there is no simple answer. This is not to say that all lures work equally well – they do not. The standard texts on the subject will all recommend the same sort of things – Redgills, Eddystones, Tobys, and so on. You need to consider what the fish are likely to be feeding on and how to reach the feeding area and depth. The problem of imitating a particular item of food can be considered in several separate parts:

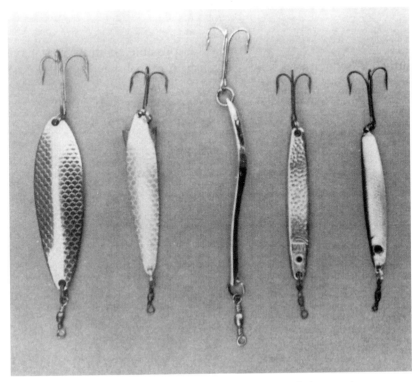

Useful spoon-type lures for long-distance or teeth-of-the-wind spinning. Left to right: Koster, Toby, German sprat, Krill and heavy lead-based lure which can be bent to change its action.

1.   Movement – fast or slow, smooth or jerky, up, down or level, towards or away from cover.
2.   Size.
3.   Shape – long and thin, short and fat, round or flat.
4.   Colour – shade, markings, contrast, flash.

Perhaps the best way to illustrate how to approach these choices is to take an example. Isle of Wight bass often feed on wrasse. Presumably the size of the wrasse eaten varies but, for the sake of argument, we can assume that they are often from three to four inches long. Now wrasse of all species are deep-bodied, brightly coloured fish with slow deliberate movements. The commonest small inshore forms – the corkwing, rock-cook and the young of

Sole-skin lure, seldom used these days, but still very effective.

the ballan – are usually bronze-brown or greenish-brown in colour. We are looking for a lure giving the impression of a short, fat, slow-moving, brownish creature, so what are the possibilities? A simple spoon, a bar spoon, a fat-sprat Devon, a Fat-Rap, Big-S or Hi-Lo-style plug. Any of these could have a copper, bronze or brown painted finish and could be fished quite slowly, near rock or weed cover.

It is odds on that the fish will be close in, so there should be no problem reaching them, even with a lightweight lure. The conditions are likely to be snag-ridden wrasse territory, so fast-sinking metal lures could be prone to plunge to their doom. Bass usually take their prey with a side swipe, so a hook mid-body is generally effective; however, a 3- or 4-inch lure is liable to be engulfed, so hooking should be no problem. Fast reeling keeps lures (except plugs) high in the water, but this is not consistent with the slow-moving behaviour of the wrasse, so how else can they be prevented from sinking? A float is one possibility, but that is a bit clumsy. Nonetheless, float-spinning is widely practised by bass anglers. Bar spoons can be fitted with buoyant polystyrene or balsa-wood bodies. Devon minnows (rarely used for sea fishing) include wooden, plastic and rubber forms. Only the lighter types are worthy of consideration and, if you want a wrasse-like Devon, you will have to make it yourself. This is no great problem,

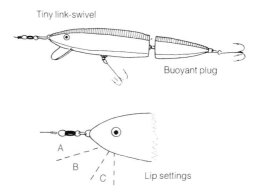

Lip settings on a buoyant plug: A, deep dive; B, medium dive and lively action; C, near-surface swim for fast-flowing shallow water.

Tiny link-swivel

Buoyant plug

Lip settings

even for the do-it-yourself duffer (and believe me, I am the worst).

Plugs can be bought or made and rendered as wrasse-like as you wish. Again, there is the choice of buoyant and slow- or fast-sinking lures. Except in deep water or over clean seabeds, the latter are money wasted. Plugs dive shallowly or steeply according to the setting of the lip. A floating plug has most of the characteristics required of an imitation wrasse and would be my own choice because of its versatility. This hypothetical case shows the proper approach to the problem.

In the south-west approaches off the coast of Devon and Cornwall, sandeels are often the premier bass food. Again the choice of lures is quite wide, but in this case the fish are looking for a long, slim 'silver pencil', shimmering and darting along somewhere between the surface of the open sea and the ripple-marked sandy bed. It is no accident that the Redgill was developed down in the clear Cornish waters. The original rubber eel, simply a piece of rubber tube cut to give it a tail and pushed on to a suitable hook, was superseded by translucent Porosands and silver two-piece Mevagisseys before the wagging, soft-bodied Redgills and Eddystones made their appearance. These lures, with their built-in fishy-type swimming motion, are about as close to the natural eel as could be imagined.

The soft rubber eel can be fished without added weight. Simply rig it with heavy nylon so that a small swivel is tight to the nose; it can then be tied direct to the line or clipped on like any other lure.

Because they are so light, silicone-rubber eels must be fished very slowly to keep them at any appreciable depth. Weight, in the form of a barrel lead, can be added up-trace or inside the eel. The

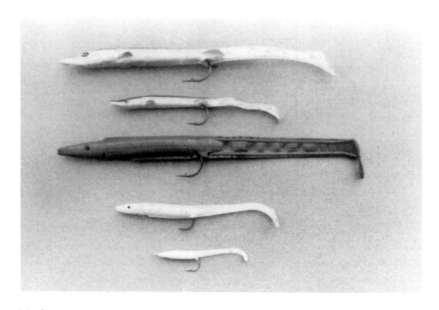

Modern sandeel imitations. Top to bottom: large and small Redgills, Eddystone, small and very small Delta eels.

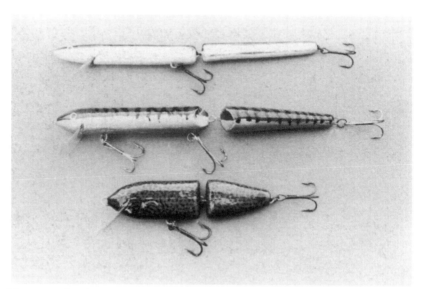

Home-made plugs fashioned to represent sandeel, mackerel and small wrasse.

An assortment of shop-bought floating plugs. The Rapala and the Nils Master (top and middle left) are more expensive but reliable products.

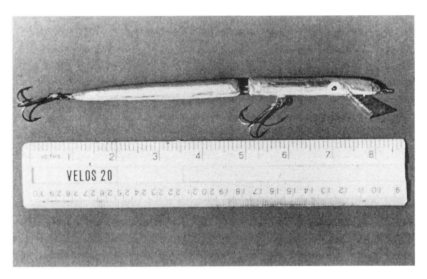

A successful home-made balsa plug in the form of a sandeel.

The big mouth of a plug-caught eight-pounder.

normal hook fitted to these lures is rather large and coarse, though often sharp. If you favour a finer wire hook, it is possible to replace the original. It may, however, be necessary to pad the hook shank to keep it neatly in the mid-line or to rig the lure with a double hook for stability. The buoyancy and rigging of the eel can be delicately adjusted to the needs of any given fishing situation.

Quite a few other lures are pretty good imitations of sandeels. The old German sprat and its modern pirk and Toby counterparts are very effective means of reaching extreme (100 yards or more) distance, jigging in deep, fast-flowing water or pushing out against an onshore gale. Their actions leave something to be desired and they may require more rod work to give them life. Toby spoons and their cheaper imitations are all pretty good sandeel replicas and have quite an edge in windy conditions, with the advantage of a fine, flickering wobble on the retrieve or against the flow. Long thin Devons have possibilities, but the hook at the rear end is not so good for bass.

Slim, single-jointed and two-jointed floating plugs, such as Rapalas, are pretty good artificial eels, but they are suitable only for short casting or for situations where the current or the boat movement will carry them away and impart a suitable action to

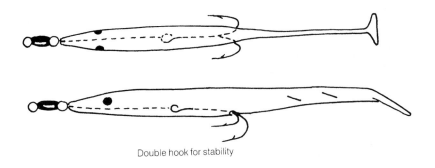

Double hook for stability

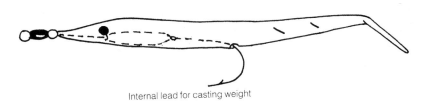

Internal lead for casting weight

Silicone-rubber eels modified to give swimming stability or with internal weight for distance fishing.

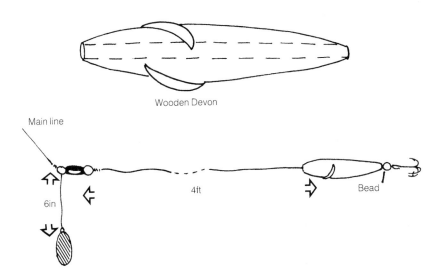

Wooden Devon

Main line

4ft

Bead

6in

Simple construction and fishing rig for a wooden Devon minnow.

85

A 12½lb fish hooked on a Rebel J30S slides ashore.

them. I have seen sessions where sandeel-feeding bass struck at a Redgill fished by my son about three times as often as at a J-11 Rapala fished by me, but the latter hooked just as many fish as the former. If you object to the many trebles on plugs, it is possible to clip off some of the points without ill effect.

One last essential for spinning, as for bottom fishing, is some means of landing your hard-earned fish. My personal preference is for a gaff, which, unlike a net, does not tangle with the trebles on a lure. In practice most of my bass are beached and lifted out by hand, but when a fish is especially large or important I have no hesitation in using the gaff. A net is a useful alternative if you are prepared to spend often vital minutes untangling hooks and meshes. For mobility in spinning, a light, folding net of the type used by trout fly fishermen is very handy.

In conclusion, whether bottom-fishing or spinning for bass, certain general principles must not be lost sight of. First, many of the fish are taken in very shallow water, close to the shore. Second, it is worth trying to minimise the effects of tackle shyness by using little or no weight and lines strong enough to cope with the conditions but no stronger. Third, on static, bottom-fished baits, bass often take slowly, but on moving baits, notably spun lures or sometimes baits swept about by wave action, the takes will usually be ferocious. These are just two sides of the fish's character. Lastly, hooks must be as sharp as possible at all times, and striking must be very positive.

In recent years a number of additional lures have been developed for bass fishing; some of these are very good and others are useful in very special circumstances. Details are given in Chapter 13, which deals with new developments.

FLY FISHING

ML   There are occasions when neither bait nor spinning tactics will persuade the bass to show any interest. When the fish are obsessed with tiny fry, fish larvae, small squid, shrimps, slaters, maggots or small swimming worms it may prove difficult or even impossible to present a small enough natural bait in such a way that it will attract or deceive them. Freshwater game fishermen have faced a similar problem for a great many years. Their main quarry, various species of trout, feed to a large extent on small insects and crustaceans. The secret of deceiving fish preoccupied with these tiny specks of life is to present them with a small, essentially weightless lure, and the best method of projecting such lures to the fish is to use fly tackle in which the casting weight is supplied by the thick, heavy line.

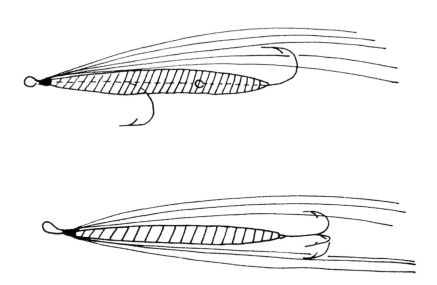

Streamer flies – effective when fished on fly tackle for fry-feeding bass.

The back-and-forth switching action which is needed to cast with fly gear is much too violent for use with most natural baits. Only tough materials such as squid, mackerel strip or old, leathery, bluebottle maggots will stay on the hook for long enough to make them a proposition. Artificial 'flies' designed to imitate small swimming creatures are legion, but few of them were tied with bass food in mind. The basic principle of representing size, shape, colour and movement apply, just as they do in spinning. For guidance, the fry flies, terrors, streamers, polystickles, chompers, baby dolls, appetisers and so on which tempt large predatory trout are reasonable choices for many bass-fishing situations. Observe, think, tie and try is the best approach.

What sort of fly rods, reels and lines are suitable for bass angling? Unless you have a special place and set of conditions in mind (in which case you will know what you want) it is probably best to go for versatility. Much of the fishing is likely to be with wet (sub-surface) flies and the fish you are after will be somewhere between a trout and a salmon in size and packed with fight. Rods of the type designed for sea trout or for reservoir trout fishing are probably about right. Rods from 9 to 11 feet in length designed to cast line weights between number 6 and number 9 will cope with most conditions and allow for the odd occasion when a dry fly is appropriate (or when you fancy a crack at some surface-feeding mullet). A floating line is probably most versatile but a spare spool with a sink-tip can occasionally be useful if the fish are a few feet down.

Most fly reels are made of aluminium or aluminium alloy and unless they are looked after well are likely to corrode quickly. Since the reel is mainly a store for the bulky line it is probably pointless to buy the luxury models. There are one or two plastic or carbon-fibre fly reels on the market which should be ideal for sea angling but I have never aspired to buy one and, in practice, I have only got through two ordinary alloy reels in about fifteen years of intensive fishing.

Fly fishing for bass is mostly aimed at presenting a small lure within a few feet of the sea surface, where the fish will be seeking small fry, particularly around the periods of dusk and dawn. While a floating line or a sink-tip will often be suitable, every situation should be considered on its merits. Since it is mainly the smaller school bass which feed on sandhoppers, slaters and the like, it will be in estuaries, lagoons and shallow muddy harbours that the fly tackle can be wielded with a fair chance of sport.

Sheltered Ledge. Note the kelp, which can be successfully fished with a light leger tackle.

However, big bass will also take a fly and on some occasions it may be not simply the best way of catching fish but the only tactic which will lure a decent specimen.

Don't be tempted to use big, crude hooks dressed to resemble Christmas tree decorations. If these will catch fish then, almost certainly, spinning lures or bait will be better. It is when hefty bass are hell-bent on abundant small creatures that the fly will be most effective. Flies such as Clouser Minnows and Deceivers, tied with predominantly white and silver hair, are appropriate, and I often use small white Delta eels in lieu of flies. If a long-bodied fly is needed to represent, say, a juvenile sandeel, then tandem size 10 hooks will give better penetration and a very secure hold on the largest fish. Believe me, the flexibility of a fly rod and the damping effect of a fly line, combined with a sensitive hand on the reel, will beat any bass that swims.

5
Shallow Rocky Shores

All the bass were taken in very shallow water, within a few feet of the reef and quite at the shore end of it.

F. B. Hannam, *B.S.A.S. Quarterly*, 1922

Shallow rocks and reefs attract and hold bass, especially bigger bass. Some of the reasons are easy to find: rocks often provide an anchorage for seaweeds, and seaweeds provide both food and shelter for a variety of marine creatures which are the food for a wide range of larger animals, including bass. The principal foods of big bass are crabs and smaller fish, both of which are abundant in and near rocky areas. Larger bass spend much of their time in *selected* rocky areas, to the extent of being territorial in those places.

Alan has caught several fish twice in a particular place. On one occasion, when fishing from Friar's Point in Barry, he lost a fish through the line breaking only to retrieve his hook and characteristic elastic bands from the same fish when he hooked and this time landed it from almost exactly the same position two days later.

Smaller bass would probably be under some threat from their bigger relations if they spent a lot of time over reefs. This may be part of the reason why fewer small bass are caught on the rocks. Equally important may be their need for shelter from the strong currents, and for particular foods which are more readily available in other places. Whatever the reasons, the average size of bass over rocky ground is usually between 3 and 5lb.

SEARCHING OUT THE FISH

ML The natural prey items which live over rocky platforms and ledges include many active, fast swimmers such as 'rockfish', squat lobsters and prawns. In a strong tidal flow, over a hard bottom,

Anticipation – could it be a bass picking up the king rag bait?

No – it was only a ballan wrasse.

the bass will be on the look-out for this type of animal and the angler should be prepared to make the most of the search images which these fish acquire.

Spinning with natural or artificial baits involves more or less constant casting and retrieving. Because of this, it is an excellent way of representing lively animals. The use of natural spinning baits is really no more than a way of imparting a bit more movement (and possibly more appropriate movement) than would be achieved by legering or float fishing. Over shallow, snag-ridden, abrasive, rocky bottoms it is often a great advantage to use artificials.

Before you close this book at the mere thought of flinging your 'gold-plated', highly valued lures into impenetrable masses of rock and weed, consider three things. First, how much time or money do you spend on bait every year? Second, it is possible to make excellent lures quite cheaply. Third, and more important, the object of spinning artificials over rock is to catch bass while avoiding contact with natural hazards. There are essentially two

Wrack and boulders which yield bass to buoyant plugs at high water.

ways of keeping spinning lures near the water surface. One is to use sinking baits (metal spoons, etc.) and reel in quickly. This does not take account of overruns, miscasts or misjudgement of water depth, any of which can result in an expensive twang of the line. The other is to use strategies which prevent the lure sinking. These include the various forms of float-spinning, with the attractor suspended beneath some sort of buoyancy aid. Rather easier is the use of buoyant plugs, lightweight spinners, rubber eels or flies.

In spinning over shallow rocky areas it is often possible to catch bass on any phase or at any state of the tide, but, as with bottom-fished baits, quite often the fish bite best on the flood. When breaking new ground it probably pays to fish only short sessions at each venue, taking careful note on every trip of the tide, conditions and time of day. This is my approach and establishing the best time for any spot has often involved many hours of frequently fruitless angling.

Every bass angler should first consider how to prospect an unfamiliar area quickly. What is likely to be the most rapid means of covering the ground – and the fish? Which method involves the maximum amount of bait movement? Which method or methods

A 4½lb bass is easily beached on an 8lb line.

permit the angler to fish over and cover unknown, unseen ground without snagging? Which method is likely to induce the bass to reveal their presence by moving, or showing themselves, or giving a tug, tap, pull or pluck on the tackle, or even hooking themselves. Which method allows the angler a high degree of mobility in his search and enables him to present a range of desirable foods to the bass without time spent bait collecting? Which method minimises the number of nuisance bites from small fish of other species?

All of these characteristics can be achieved by spinning with low-density or buoyant baits, notably plugs in a variety of shapes and sizes. Bass, large and small, will follow and take plugs; in many respects they present the ideal approach for an angler on an unknown stretch of coastline with limited time at his disposal.

For example, on a week's holiday in an unfamiliar area where 40-foot tides are the rule and bass are known to be abundant, I was having a thin time. The weather had been good – from the family's point of view – but the fishing had been a flop. Despite collecting razorfish, digging worms, catching crabs and prawns and spending as many hours as I could (mostly late evening and early morning) fishing harbours, sandy strands and rocky gullies, no bass were forthcoming. Day after day the sun blazed from the cloudless sky, the sea was flat calm and the water was as clear as crystal. When the sun shone, small wrasse gorged themselves on my crab and prawn baits and, as dusk fell, even smaller pollack fell upon the worms with gay abandon, but not a prickle of a bass showed itself.

On the Thursday evening before we were due to return home, the family decided, in an attempt to keep Dad sane, to visit a rocky headland fully exposed to the south-west. The Friday came, as everyone but myself had hoped, without a breath of wind and with the sun blazing down from a cloudless sky. We parked the car and made our way into a rocky sun-trap facing the sea. Everyone promptly set about their business of sunbathing, stone turning, rock-pool dabbling, climbing or exploring. I perched myself on a handy rock and stared at the sea.

As always, my rod and reel lay on the rocks, crowning a pile of towels, food and other sundry seaside items. After a while, I decided to give it a go, though the prospects were not encouraging. Taking the rod, I attached a home-made eight-inch balsa sandeel plug to the 8lb line and walked across the rugged surface towards the water's edge. The heat of the rock warmed my feet through the thin rubber of my plimsolls. The tide was well in and flooding over the rocky platform above mid-tide level. By standing on a slight ridge, a couple of feet above the surrounding rocks, I could see, with the aid of polaroids, every limpet and tuft of weed. Most of the underwater platform was clothed in a couple of inches of bright green algae with the appearance of freshwater blanket-weed. The back of my plug was, by chance, painted about the same colour as the weed so, as I retrieved it just below the surface, it was practically invisible until it was almost at my feet. I flicked it out and wound it back two or three times, trying to spread the casts to cover every minor variation in the seabed.

A slight sea breeze had developed and was blowing from my right, so on the fourth cast I tossed the plug high in the air and to my left to gain an extra yard or two of distance. It plopped lightly on to the calm surface about ten yards from the water's edge and submerged as I began to reel in. Every second or two I would catch a glint of its silver-papered flank as it wriggled sinuously through the water. Quite suddenly I became aware of two grey shapes just behind the plug and, before my mind could register 'bass', the rod was almost pulled from my hands by a fierce take.

The clear water swirled violently as, five yards to my left, the fish turned away, having hooked itself firmly on the middle treble. It surged away out to sea, with the carp rod well bent, taking line against the firm clutch in a series of strong rushes. Characteristically, the bass sheared back and forth after being brought to a halt by the steady pressure of the line. After a couple of minutes of give and take, I stooped and lifted the 4½lb fish from the water, gripping it firmly behind the head and taking care to avoid the trebles as the fish wagged its suspended body strongly from side to side. I pinned it down, removed the hooks with my artery forceps and slid it back into the sea, watching until it was out of sight.

I picked up the rod and cast again in more or less the same direction. I could not believe my eyes when another grey shape appeared behind the plug and again followed it for some distance, in full view, before making a side-swiping grab at the slim, jointed sliver of wood. The battle was repeated in almost every detail and a second bass was unhooked and returned. In the following half-hour, I had one more bass of about the same size, then I packed in and walked up the shore for a final soaking of sunshine.

Now, had I been using bait, I could well have caught the same or even more or bigger fish, but the point to note is the simplicity of the approach. Had I been alone and in other circumstances I could have covered several miles of shoreline, casting and retrieving, confident in the knowledge that there was a good chance of action. Even if you do not catch a bass on such a search mission it is quite rare not to learn something about the movements or activity of the fish. So what do you look for?

Bass taking lures in shallow, rocky areas are generally (though not always) hunting for small fish. The prey are rarely far from cover so fish over or near boulders, ledges and wrack or kelp beds. In my part of Dorset it is not unusual to see the bass lunge on to a lure from behind a patch of bladder-wrack, within a few yards of the water's edge. On shallow rocks the fish will follow the tide in, hunting through the shallow pools which may be depressions only a foot or so below the level of the surrounding plateau. The bottom of such pools will usually be covered with pink coralline algae and tufts of small brown seaweeds. They are the places where, at low water, blennies and bullheads (sea scorpions) shelter, and the bass are well aware of this. I have hooked large bass literally at my feet in the turmoil of white water caused by a wave crashing into such a rock pool as the tide rose. So there is the first clue: look for slight irregularities in the rocky seabed.

Are there any other clues which might suggest the presence of bass? Birds of any sort should never be ignored. Some, such as waders – notably oystercatchers, purple sandpipers, and so on – indicate the presence of potential bass foods such as crabs or molluscs. Others, like gulls of various types, are real opportunists. Large crowds of gulls squabbling at the water's edge usually show that there is some source of easy pickings – sandhoppers, slaters, maggots or rubbish cast up by the waves. At some stage the bass will take advantage of the same food source when the tide makes it available.

The best sign of all for the bass spinner is a fishing bird. Gulls, being versatile, will plunge-dive for near surface food. Normally they are not very good at this type of fishing but, when underwater predators disorient shoals of brit or sandeels (these little fish can be almost as common over rock as over sand), then the old squawkers will make hay. Terns are much more efficient fishers and can catch the fry as they go about their normal business. The same applies to subsurface hunters like shags, guillemots, razor-bills and puffins, so never ignore even a single feeding bird. It does not need to be a screaming horde of feathered predators to indicate the presence of fish. The effect of the birds is twofold from the angler's point of view. First, they always show where the fish are *likely* to be. Second, by working a sort of pincer movement with the bass, each makes it easier for the other to catch prey.

Cormorants, perhaps the commonest fishing birds we encounter, tend to feed on wrasse in rocky areas and will swallow quite large specimens of over a pound in weight. They are not, in my experience, very good indicators of bass activity, but don't take my view as gospel. Bass will also feed avidly on wrasse if they can catch them, and are certainly likely to be in the same areas as feeding cormorants.

The episode described in Chapter 12 was associated with plunging terns and gulls and no bass angler can afford to ignore these signs.

So how do you know whether the rod-jarring knock or pluck on your lure was a fish or not? First, if the lure comes back with any scraps of weed or rubbish on the hooks, swivel or vane, it is probable that what you felt was weed. If the knock is repeated in

Mike with a fine catch of fish to 9½lb caught on J11 Rapala.

Phil Williams with a beautifully conditioned fish of 10lb 3oz
caught in a near-gale and heavy rain. The fish was sixteen
years old.

David Williams with a 12lb 3oz bass caught from a sandy
beach. An 11-foot carp rod, fixed-spool reel and 1oz lead
were used to cast out mackerel fillet bait.

Deeper water bass – Alan with a fish of 12¼lb and Phil Williams with one of 10½lb.

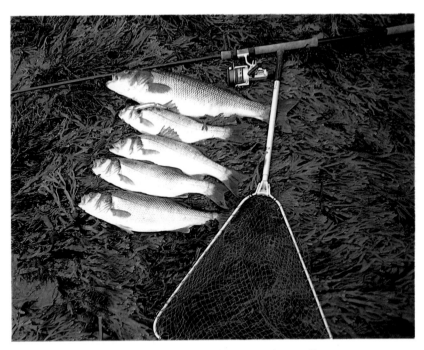

Bass caught on buoyant plugs – weights range from 4lb 4oz to 9lb 9oz.

Mike and Martin Williams with fish of 10½ and 4½lb, caught in June from shallow water.

A small strand in Brandon Bay, Eire. Bass were caught from just behind the wave about twenty yards out.

Kelp jungle at St Helens, Isle of Wight. This type of ground should be sought out, not avoided, by the bass angler.

A decent bass is given a helping hand into shallow, weedy water.

Harry Casey spinning a buoyant plug for bass.

A view from the hot-spot of Quiet Bay taken during the flood tide.

Alan unhooking a 7¾lb bass on a shallow, rocky ledge near Barry, South Wales.

Martin Giddy holds a typical juvenile fish caught at Aberthaw using a Delta eel and Jif lemon rig. Fish of less than 3lb or so should always be returned, as this one was.

the same spot on the next retrieve and does not result in a fish, it is quite likely to be a slight ridge in the rocky seabed. If your floating plug hangs up solid in the rocks, what do you do? Slack off and it will probably free itself. Because they are buoyant, these lures tend to pop to the surface and, in doing so, will often release the hook which has simply lodged on a sharp edge or projection of rock. If it catches in weed then 10lb BS line will generally pull it free, particularly if it has razor-sharp hooks to slice through the leathery fronds. Try pulling from a different angle – slacking off between pulls – and this will sometimes release a firmly wedged hook from a ridge of rock. Never pull with the rod because the lure is likely to twang free and the spring of the rod will catapult it at high velocity, hooks and all, back towards you. As a last resort, a steady pull with the line wrapped round a smooth piece of wood or similar material, a gloved hand, or a well-padded sleeve will often free an expensive lure.

Bass almost always take a plug with what appears to be great ferocity, and you are left in no doubt of what has happened. Plucks and taps may often be felt as a result of other fish having a

Martin Williams fishes for bass using a plug over a shallow rocky ledge.

Seven plug-caught beauties landed in a brief autumn session from a shallow rocky ledge.

These three bass, the largest at 9½lb, were the result of early experiments with plugs.

go. Pollack will often take with a similar fierce yank to that of a bass. Wrasse and mullet, however, particularly smallish ones, will pluck and tug at the tail treble and may avoid being hooked, so just maintain a steady retrieve in the hope that they will take a better grip and reveal their nature.

Lastly, keep your eyes open. Just as in coarse or game fishing, a bulge of water behind the plug, a swirl close by, a flash of silver-bronze gill cover or flank, a glimpse of a prickly, erect dorsal fin or the projecting lobe of a powerful tail will give away the presence of a fish. Such events are commonplace to the keen-eyed bass angler. I consider it a very unusual trip if I do not see such signs. At times the fish will even leave the water completely in their chase and I well remember watching my plug, blown across the surface by a gale of wind, being chased by a good bass, which repeatedly left the water in its attempts to catch the 'little fish' playing at ducks and drakes.

Martin Williams returns for breakfast with a plug-caught fish of 10½lb.

If the water is calm and clear, keep a weather eye open for 'followers'. These are fish which seem unable to make up their minds about the lure and may follow it right to the water's edge. As an example, my pal Dave Cooling was spinning over shallow, boulder-strewn rocks when he saw a large fish following the Rebel plug. He kept his calm (quite unlike me) and continued reeling. As the plug neared the margin, its path crossed a huge grey rock covered by only a couple of inches of water. He thought that his chance had gone, but no, the bass followed, grounding itself on top of the boulder and taking the lure as it did so, before thrashing its way back into deeper water well hooked. It is usually easy to distinguish the grey, torpedo-shaped body of a following bass from the olive-green polaris of a pollack or the mahogany airship of a wrasse.

The behaviour of small prey fish will also reveal areas where bass are likely to be feeding. The tiny moving wrinkles caused by subsurface shoals of sand-smelts, sandeels or brit can often be seen in calm conditions. As the plug wriggles beneath them, they will scatter in a mini-flash-expansion from the surface. At such times it is often easy to determine just what the little fish are. Larger groups of spraying fry not associated with your own activities are almost always a sign of predator activity and, in the shallow rocky areas, the predators are usually bass, so get that lure or bait out to them at once.

Having throroughly explored the shallow rocks, by careful observation and persistent spinning, it is probable that you will reach the same conclusions as many other bass anglers. These suggest that the best areas to fish are those with a large extent of flattish rocks. Bass are to be taken over small isolated patches of rock certainly, but the biggest populations and most reliable fishing seem to be where there are extensive 'pavements'. Deeper water over hard bottoms makes it more likely that other fish, for example conger or pollack, will be present and less likely that the bass will be there. Probably, inshore feeding bass prefer the shallows and elsewhere they are unable to compete so well with other fish. Whatever the reasons, bass fill the role of predator-in-chief over shallow rocks in the warmer waters of the south and west coasts.

It is not always possible or desirable to spin with buoyant lures over the rough. Other methods will take either more or bigger bass in certain circumstances. Strong onshore winds will hamper the casting of unleaded tackle so much that a heavy, slim spoon or even a small pirk, retrieved at speed, may be the only way to reach the fish. Sandeel feeders will often prefer a tiny Redgill or a silver streamer-fly and, particularly in coloured or turbulent water, a big, bottom-fished bait will be most successful in picking out real hefty specimens. As with the tides, all kinds of wind strengths and directions should be fished until it becomes obvious which is best. I know of one spot in which calm to moderate conditions produce fish on top of a flat rocky ledge while in rough conditions the fish move off the ledge into the lee-side gully, where they will take a plug with gay abandon in the white foaming water over a kelpy boulder reef. This applies until the water becomes unfishable with silt, sand and fragments of floating debris, or until the wind is so strong that it is impossible to cast or keep a lure in the water.

Float fishing is also a useful method of catching bass over rough ground. It has the great advantage over bottom-fishing methods that it effectively keeps the baited hook clear of weed and snags, so relatively fine tackle can be used. Ten- or twelve-pound line is generally enough to cope with most conditions. Baits suspended from a float can be placed in situations where they are easily seen by the fish and, with skilful casting and use of wind, currents, wave action and bait activity, they can be made to cover a lot of ground – perhaps more than is possible by any other method.

Float tackle is often used to fish gullies and rock edges from vantage points some distance above the water. As the tide floods into such places, a float-fished prawn or live fish bait can be allowed to work its way into the potential feeding area. The Portland locals fish with sand-smelts or chunks of mackerel close to the rock faces of the Dorset hot-spots.

Twenty-five years ago Bob Sprawling, one of my pals, was at college in Swansea. Bob was always a keen angler and I remember clearly his description of catching an 8lb bass on float tackle. He had simply modelled his approach on that of the locals, which was to suspend a peeler crab on a treble hook beneath a decent-sized float and let it drift in the rocky gullies as the tide flooded into them. It struck me at the time that few things could seem less natural than a ball of crab meat dangling from the surface and bobbing about in the surface chop. Naturalness is obviously not essential to this bass-fishing method, but, to make the most of the

Many hands make light work when removing a multi-hooked plug from a big bass.

float technique, it would seem best to use either swimming animals or baits which look like swimming animals.

Apart from living prawns, shrimps, wrasse, pouting and so on, all of which are appropriate and successful bass attractors, it may be more convenient to use dead crabs and other baits or even artificials under a float. The use of Redgills with big floats or Jif lemons is described in Chapter 6 and there seems to be no reason why scaled-down versions should not be employed where conditions are less extreme. Strips of mackerel, fillets of sandeel, slivers of squid or whole ragworm, all hooked to 'hang loose', look very alive in the water. The method to employ is to drop the float in a position from which it will be carried into the feeding area. At intervals, the float should be held back, causing the bait to swim up towards the surface. This will often induce a bass to bite. If any weight is needed for casting (and this is quite rare over shallow rocky ground) it should mostly be concentrated in or near the float.

The main problem with float-fished baits is that floats are a compromise between visibility, support of tackle, and resistance to the pull of the taking fish. For all their hefty appearance, bass can be quite sensitive to drag and I have seen fish repeatedly grab a bait and release it after carrying the gear for two or three feet. To make a small float more conspicuous a set of vanes can be glued on top without adding much resistance to the taking fish. Thought should also be given to the hooking properties at the business end of the tackle. Single hooks should generally be short-shanked, wide-gaped and left (as always) with plenty of point exposed. The use of a pair of trebles, with the more bulky baits, could also be explored.

FOLLOWING UP THE SEARCH

AV Fishing with a bait on the bottom over snaggy ground presents difficulties in tackle loss and the playing and landing of fish. However, legering is often a very good way of catching larger specimens from rocky areas.

Sheltered rocky coasts usually have a luxuriant growth of seaweed and therefore a rich food supply; also, the water is likely

Alan with a 9½lb Gower bass caught on crab in a rough sea over shallow rocks, in late October.

to be calmer. In these places bass move in with the tide to a timetable of their own, made for each particular set of rocks. If you catch a bass in a gully at a certain state of the tide, it is ten to one that you will be able to repeat your success on other occasions. Indeed, during the season the only thing that seems to interrupt the pattern on sheltered coasts is very rough weather. Heavy seas can also make fishing such places almost impossible, since moving and drifting weed makes the use of any method very difficult.

On such a weedy, rocky coast, the bottom fishing is usually very good following rough weather *as soon as the floating weed subsides*. The water is still rather murky and the fishing stays good until it clears, which can take several days of calm weather. Of course it may be possible to find a place where there is less drifting weed and then good catches can be made (Quiet Bay is a good example – see Chapter 11).

On more exposed rocks there will be less weed, since wave action either prohibits or curtails the growth of many seaweeds. Exposed rocks, with less weed growing, tend to have less food for bass. However, there is usually some potential food sheltering in cracks and crevices. For example, edible and velvet fiddler crabs may be there, and also small fish. These animals become available as food to the bass when rough weather dislodges them. Over exposed rocks in moderately rough weather with a surf, the bass will feed keenly, and these rocks can be fished successfully in white-water conditions, since drifting weed is less likely to be a problem.

In my experience the best general conditions for rough-ground legering are when the water is not clear; a slight rippling of the surface or distinct waves also improves the situation. Provided the water is not clear, legering can be successful in daylight as well as darkness. Indeed, I have detected little difference in catches made under these conditions by day or by night. My favourite time is at first light and just after. When the water is clear it is advantageous to fish at night or when the sky is overcast, but night fishing with bait in very clear water will still be generally worse than daylight fishing in more murky seas. Clear water certainly makes legering a dodgy proposition, especially if the sea is calm, although moving the bait can be effective in inducing bass to take. The worst possible situation is settled weather, a gin-clear sea, flat calm and a bright sun. Most fish under these conditions are more likely to be chasing shoals of small fish, and spinning or livebaiting are then more appropriate methods.

Spring tides seem to be better than neap tides in many places. However, this rule is far from being without exceptions. It is important to be clear about several factors: first, bait is easier to get on spring tides; second, some areas are only fishable during spring tides; third, the flow of water is greater during springs. Bass seem to feed better in a strong current and are then easier to catch. For these reasons the fishing is frequently better during spring tides. Most of my favourite places are spring-tide places and most of these are low-water spots, although the most consistent legering for bass I ever found (a place I call Quiet Bay – it has no real name) was a high-water spring place. I have also known several good neap-tide places, so neap tides need not be ruled out, especially if you have a supply of frozen crab bait, collected during spring low tides.

To illustrate some points I will describe a trip to Quiet Bay:

My wife, Lesley, knew only too well that an early trip to the pub and an early return home, during our August holiday on the Isle of Wight, heralded my departure on a night bass-fishing trip. Patiently she observed me collecting the frozen wrasse from the freezer and the bucket of soft and peeler shore crabs from the empty coal bunker (crabs that Lesley had helped me collect, bless her).

As I left the house I knew that conditions would be good at Bonchurch that night. There was no wind to speak of, but the water was still coloured from a blow several days before. The little wind there was came from the west, so the rocky beach I intended to fish would not have rough water coming in (rough water made fishing extremely difficult and dangerous where I was going). It was dark, and I had one hour to get to Bonchurch and twenty minutes to walk along the beach to the bay I had discovered five years earlier, where bass arrived so predictably at high water on spring tides in suitable conditions. The car journey was uneventful and, after parking at the top of the cliff, I was relieved to see just a small swell breaking at the cliff base.

Pulling on my waders, I became used to the darkness and tested my torch, tied round my neck on a thick cord, where it gave a beam in the exact place I seemed to be looking when walking or landing a fish. Carefully I walked and climbed along the beach, round the corner to where Quiet Bay was waiting. Hot now from the walk, and a little tired, I put down my rucksack, the bucket of bait, rod and rod rest. The rod was a light 11-foot beach rod and I would be able to use 3oz of lead on the running leger until high water approached. After that the current would become so fierce that I would increase to 5oz, not really 'nice' fishing but by then the best time would be gone and the ebb well under way. I would be cut off by the tide and just waiting for the water to strip back far enough for me to return. The fishing here was from HW−1½ to HW+1 and long experience had shown that if there were to be any bass they arrived promptly fifteen or twenty minutes after one certain rock was submerged. Using my torch to tackle up, I was irritated by the flies, which for some reason found me more attractive than the seaweed cast up on the shore.

I had baited up and the rock was nearly gone so I made my first cast. I was not expecting anything yet, so the bait was acceptable but not special – two crisp shore crabs, a bit on the small side, were hanging three feet from the lead. Holding the rod and line and concentrating on the tension of the line took my mind away from the overhanging cliffs, which worried me, since, although I had not witnessed a rock fall, they occurred frequently. I was well away from the cliff, but later on I would be forced much closer in by the incoming tide. Nothing on that cast, so I rebaited, again with crab.

Fifteen minutes after the rock vanished I had a bite, a double pluck followed by some slack. Walking up the beach, I felt contact again, then more slack. I reeled in till I felt the fish again, twitching the bait it seemed. There was a hard pull, which I struck, but there was no resistance. This happened very quickly and, since my strike brought no contact, the fish might possibly have returned. However, there was no further movement; the bait could have been spoiled, so I reeled in. Part of the bait was missing and adrenalin was having its effect now; my heart was beating fast and the unstable cliff might have been a million miles away. All I had in my mind was putting on a good bait and recasting. The bait was about sixty yards out, since at this stage in the tide a reasonable cast was needed; later thirty yards would do.

At high water minus one hour, I felt another tug. I gave slack line and the answering pull was followed by an automatic strike. It felt as though I was hard into the rocky bottom, but then the rod bent over and the plunging resistance of a bass could be felt. A spirited pull was given and I eased the drag on the multiplier reel: if it was a big fish it would take line. However, this was a small fish and after a brief struggle a bass of about 3½lb was pulled ashore. I returned the fish, rebaited and cast out.

Almost immediately I caught a three-bearded rockling of 8oz which, typically, had taken the hook right down. I killed this doomed fish and kept it with my wrasse, since it might well be useful as bait. At half an hour before the top of the tide I had another slack-line bite on a crab bait. After taking up one lot of slack, a tug was felt and then a hard pull, which I reacted to. This time the fish fought hard and I did not know its size; it took line as it approached the shoreline, made a short run, and then I had it splashing in the surf. It ran strongly to the left, as all the bass did here (I never knew why), and then I had it on the beach. This was a fish of about 5lb and I kept it after giving it a mighty whack on the head. It seemed that this might be a good night. The water was now well up the shore and, since I did not want to be caught against the cliff, I walked hurriedly into Next Bay and made another cast. This was very snaggy ground and there was now a strong current so the line was pulling hard against my index finger. There was a fifty-fifty chance of getting this lot of tackle back – unless I hooked a fish. Just before high water I hooked another fish on crab. I was persisting with crab since it seemed to be doing well tonight. This fish was a bass of 4½lb and I returned it safely.

I was now faced with a choice – should I persist with crab or try a fish bait in the hope of a bigger fish. I made the typical decision and put on more crabs, since they were working well. I recast. After a few minutes I had a short double knock – an unusual bite for a bass over rocks, unless it was a small one. There was no power in the pulls. It is marvellous how experience tells one the difference between the gentle tug of a big fish and the small tug of a small fish. A few seconds later an identical double knock was given: a small fish had probably hooked itself and the double knock caused by a spirited double flap of the tail was the signal to reel in. A 1lb pouting was swiftly brought ashore. This was bleeding so I kept it, and now had no choice regarding bait. There was no way I was going to waste valuable crabs on pouting, so I took the wrasse that I had left out to thaw and cut it in half. For some reason or other I fancied the tail half, so on it went with the 5/0 hook through the root of the tail, and a gentle lob put the bait about thirty yards out. The current was fierce, and soon fishing would require a heavy lead (I had already increased to 4oz). The fish would soon be less easy to hook since there would be few of them bent on suicide; the extra resistance would mean the typical one-huge-pull type of bite which is so difficult to hit consistently.

Half an hour into the ebb I felt a slight tug, and then the weight lifted. I knew that the force of the water on the line would not encourage this fish to hang on all that long. Once it felt the resistance it would almost certainly drop the bait, so I took a chance, broke my rule, and ran up the beach to strike on a slack-line bite. How often have I sworn loudly and colourfully after doing this fruitlessly, but I was in luck: a good fish was hooked and the rod bent well over. This fish fought well and took line from the reel before I regained any; it took more line as it approached the shore and ran strongly to the left. There was no splashing – always a sign of a good bass – and then the fish went to the right. I could detect it shaking and then a splash a long way to the right, almost in Quiet Bay, made me badly want this fish which seemed determined to get away. Keeping the rod bent, I pulled the fish back and beached it. I could see it was a good bass and, on picking it up, thought it might be eight pounds. I killed it quickly and baited up again, casting without delay. There was no more action.

After another half-hour I wedged the rod in the rod rest and left it in order to weigh my fish. The rod would be safe with the butt under the stones; there was very little chance of a bass taking my wrasse now, and less chance of a conger. My biggest bass weighed 7lb 6oz; why do they always look a bit bigger when they are alive? As the tide receded I thought about the approaching dawn. Good as that time would be a few miles up the coast, it was time to go, so I packed up and trudged back to the car, with a delightful agony from the extra thirteen pounds of fish I was carrying.

This was a good but not unusual night for Quiet Bay and Next Bay. The fish arrived on time and went on time; and the average size was about 5lb. It was different in that I had also caught a rockling and a pouting; usually bass only were encountered, with an occasional conger. The gut contents of the fish were quite interesting. The 7½lb bass had a large part of a soft spider crab; the bass of 4lb 15oz contained one shore crab and the tail half of a mackerel. The pouting had a shore crab and a prawn, and the rockling a squat lobster and a shore crab. Bass on this shore contain almost any food – very often small fish of varying sorts and usually some crabs – but this was the only occasion that I had caught bass with spider crab or mackerel inside.

Two nights later I fished this spot again and caught four more fish between HW − 1 and HW + 1¼. The fish weighed 5¼lb, 4½lb, 4¼lb and 2½lb. Being on holiday, and having two fish from the previous occasion, I returned all these bass; no other species were caught.

These trips were in 1978. Incidentally, in recent years a lot of that cliff has fallen down and Quiet Bay no longer exists. Next Bay is still there, but is dangerous to fish, so sadly neither I nor anyone else is likely to fish it again. Luckily that coast also fishes at low water, but it is difficult fishing in the very rocky ground.

In many places the state of the tide tends to be crucial, mainly since particular places are only fishable at particular tidal levels, but also because bass, in my experience, often feed better on the early flood than at other times. As the water travels into gullies, the bass come with it, usually in very shallow water. Indeed, one night last year, as I was walking off a ledge, I put one foot into a 'gully' only six inches deep and actually trod on a bass of about 5lb. Bass use the gullies simply because there is water there, and as soon as the water is a few inches deep over the main body of a ledge or reef bass will swim over it and may be caught there. Freelining or float fishing may be practical in the gullies, but light legering is also good. However, the presence of gullies is not vital for good bass fishing and it is not necessary always to fish into gullies or off the edge of a submerged ledge. While the early flood is very good, I know of different places which fish best at all other states of the tide. I have found them by trying at every state of the tide and any ambitious angler should do the same on his own patch.

If the coast is made up of boulders, legering tends to be difficult and a lot of tackle is lost, but by and large the same rules apply as with flat ledges. I have found, however, that where I have fished into bouldery ground, although the fish keep to their timetables, when the sea is rough they can be late in arriving. Maybe they need deeper, relatively calmer water round large rocks when turbulence makes it hard work for them to avoid obstructions.

Something that does seem to be important is that on a large or small rocky outcrop or point bass concentrate where the current flows on to the rock; the sheltered side is rarely as good. However, just as salmon have lies where they can maintain station in areas of slack water, bass also hang in the current where it is disturbed by boulders or outcrops, in order to save energy. This is most easily seen from a pier, where bass shelter behind piles, but I have also found it quite reliable to fish next to rocky obstructions, and, if the current produces eddies, then the fish will often be there. A couple of years ago I fished a shingle beach with a vicious current. There were several groynes, and the only bass I could catch were all hooked in the slack water just behind the groynes.

The beginning of a new lateral flow often gives good fishing, provided that you are in the right place. The change of direction of current may or may not coincide with low or high water, but just after slack water is a good time to fish. Over rocks this might be because the attached weed all has to wash around into a new position, and sheltered organisms have to scuttle around to find new hidey-holes. In doing so, they become easy prey, and bass feed well then. Conversely, the actual slack water period always seems to be a poor time to fish.

In many places it will be obvious that the fish come in very close to the angler. Clearly in such places every care must be taken to avoid frightening them. Moving about, especially on the skyline, should be kept to a minimum. Splashing in calm water must be avoided at all costs.

I feel quite strongly about the use of lights at night. I have seen bass swim right up to my feet at night and I would never use a lamp like a Tilly when bass fishing. Apart from the stark contrasting light and shadow, the lamp is a hell of a nuisance when you are walking over rocks. You are blind outside the immediate beam and you can also get meths and paraffin on your hands. Far better to take one or two good torches and let your eyes get used to the darkness. I also keep the torch beam away from the water over shallow rocks because I see no point in running any risk of alarming fish.

When tackling up for fishing over rocks, I always use a running lead with a long hook-length. I am not convinced by the well-known arguments favouring a paternoster-type rig, which go something like this: 'I want to know immediately when a fish takes my bait and a paternoster with a short snood makes early warning more likely.' This is true, but the point missed is that the fish gets an early warning too. So the angler will only hook his bass if he strikes immediately, before the fish rejects the bait. So often I have felt bass fiddle about with bait for several minutes (that is a long, long time) and fish will often drop the bait when in this fiddling mood if they feel a weight. Far better to use a long trace, which gives the fish a bit more time to engulf the bait before it notices anything amiss. Don't worry about the bait washing under a rock or other obstruction. This can happen, but bass are really very good at getting hold of a bait that they want. If you must use a paternoster to a short snood, then always make it a running paternoster, I shall stick to my long traces. By all means experiment with long and short traces (definitely the best plan), but I have made up my mind. However, it would be interesting to hear from anglers who have compared these different methods.

A little story is worth telling at this point. I am sure my brother-in-law, Philip, will not mind. It covers about ten years, when we fished together many times during the annual holidays. Records show that every year I caught at least twice as many fish as Phil. Our tackle, bait, reactions, etc., were, as far as we could tell, the same, but I always used longer traces, often up to five feet long. These days Phil uses longer traces and now he does better, taking more fish, including two bass over 10lb.

If an ounce or less lead is adequate in a flattish rock area, then a barrel lead sliding on the main line is best. However, if a heavier lead is required, or if the ground is more snaggy, then I favour a lead on a link of 4–8 inches of a slightly lower breaking strain than the main line; with 15lb main line I would use 10 or 12lb line for the lead link. The trace should also be of a slightly lower breaking strain for most venues, though where tackle losses are unlikely, it can be the same strength as the main line. I have never used a long lead-link since, when developing these tactics, I twice lost big bass close in after the lead jammed between boulders. In both cases I saw the fish and, in one case, the lead-link broke, but the hook was obviously not in past the barb and slack line enabled the point to come out.

The rotten bottom theory is well known. My attitude is that I would rather get a lead back than lose it, so I don't like very light rotten bottoms. Usually a fish will lift the lead off the bottom and out of a snag, so there is not often a problem there. If you are simply wedged in the bottom, you are less likely to lose your lead if the weak link is not too 'rotten'. If the lead link is a little weaker than the main line, then you will usually break the lead link first, enabling you to get the hook, etc., back. If terminal tackle is not too much weaker than the main line then you can also cast out without the weird and wonderful extra paraphernalia (polystyrene pins, etc.) needed to give casting strength to a rotten bottom.

There is no real point in using a shock leader when rock bassing. If you get snagged, a leader means that you usually lose the lot and, since there is no need to cast far, it is better to be sensible with the main line and vary it according to the bottom. Pay no attention to those anglers who boast about using very light line when legering. Usually they have a heavy leader and they fish over sand at distance. Their tackle is unlikely to break during the actual fishing (it might in the casting, of course), particularly since the important bit, which is landing the fish, is probably achieved on the heavy leader. In flat rock areas, or over small stones and boulders, 15lb line is usually my first choice. If the bottom is jagged and covered with barnacles or mussels, then I might go up to 30lb main line with a 25lb trace. Believe me, even with a strong main line, bass are sometimes lost in foul ground, through frays.

Whatever rod or reel you use, my advice is to take up the slack and hold the line so that you can feel everything. Maximum sensitivity is achieved by pointing the rod straight down the line and by holding the line just off tight. You want to catch bass, so don't put the rod down unless you are baiting up. This approach takes a lot of concentration and I find it difficult to fish effectively in this manner for more than three or four hours. The bass themselves usually turn up for a short time, so there are bursts of activity. In some places they only turn up at one brief time; I know one exasperating place where, quite consistently, the fish are only present for about fifteen minutes on the flood, at about 1½ hours before high water. The rod must be held all the time and you must feel carefully for the indication that a fish is interested.

To illustrate the type of fishing where this consideration is all-important I can do no better than describe an early morning session at Sheltered Ledge:

I really am awful at getting up in the morning, so it is amazing that most of my best bass have been caught during dawn and early morning sessions. Usually I hear the alarm and get up, leave the house and wake up some time while walking down the beach. If I didn't get my gear together the night before, I'd forget something vital – like the rod or bait.

This particular morning, at the end of July, was a quiet, dry morning and conditions would be good for fishing at the ledge at Whitecliff. As I arrived near the path that would take me to the beach, I noticed the cool, fresh smell of early morning dew and felt the slight chill wind from the south-west – light, but enough to produce a few small waves and to cover the sea with ripples.

This was the fishing that I most enjoy – spinning rod, one ounce of lead, net and a few spare items of tackle in a rucksack. The bait would be frozen wrasse, which were kept in an expanded polystyrene cool-box that I had made to keep bait frozen for up to five hours. Crab would not be a suitable bait since where I was going to fish it was absolutely alive with wrasse of all sizes, corkwings and ballans, and crab baits would be wasted on them. Using small wrasse as bait, I would be unlikely to catch anything but bass from the shallow water I was going to fish.

I carefully walked across the sandy bay and down the ledge, avoiding the holes and stones, and noticed that there was no loose weed lying about. Two days earlier, when the wind had been stronger, weed had been cast up and was also drifting in the water. When weed catches on your line, bite detection is hopeless, the tackle gets snagged and you catch little or, more usually, nothing. Today the water would be nicely coloured, but there would be no drifting weed. Also, there was no significant wave action and the fish would be able to move in on their usual tracks in the shallow water, searching among the kelp for crabs and small fish, especially for small wrasse. When I reached the water's edge I could see that it was shallow for about twenty-five yards out, with kelp and boulders poking out of the water for the first fifteen yards. An inexperienced angler would never cast there, but I knew the fish would be moving in even now and as I arrived, a fish splashed about five yards out and snaked back away from me. I had frightened that one; I would need to be careful, but it is always good to know that the fish are there.

First of all the net was put together, then the 9-foot spinning rod assembled, already with fixed spool reel attached. The line, 15lb BS, was threaded through the rings and a 1oz barrel lead was stopped by a small split ring. A 15lb trace of 30 inches with a 5/0 hook completed the tackle. I took out three wrasse and put the smallest on the hook, fixing it through the lips. The other wrasse went into a pool to thaw.

My first cast was just over the last pieces of kelp that were above water, about twenty yards, and I carefully took up some slack, holding the line across a finger and pointing the rod straight down the line for maximum sensitivity. The current was strong and the bait was about 25 degrees to the right of the direction the line entered the water. Fish could come any time between now and when I would be 'washed off'. This was my favourite fishing. The bass are cautious and difficult to hook, giving such gentle bites, but they could be big fish; I had had quite a few seven-, eight- and nine-pounders from this ledge. Slack-line bites were common and it was necessary to be very gentle at taking up the slack. When the angler can feel the fish pull, the fish can equally feel the resistance, so, if the first indication of a fish arriving was a tug, I would push the rod forward for a yard and watch the line. If it started straightening I would be ready to strike as it tightened, but if it twitched and fell down I would need to take up the slack carefully.

On my second cast, having rebaited after the first wrasse had been severely crabbed, at 1 hour after low water, I had my first take; a tug had been followed by a pull and I had hooked a fish of 3lb. A bass of that size fights well on a light rod and I had a few anxious moments before it would allow itself to be pulled over the net. This beautiful fish put itself into a tight bend, keeping its body upright as I put down the net. The dorsal spines were standing up and the little bass seemed so affronted, so aggressive. I carefully removed the hook from the corner of its mouth and slid it back into the water; it was gone in a flash. I rebaited with my favourite bait, the belly half of a fish cut from the mouth to the root of the tail, and recast. I had an hour before I would have to move or risk being cut off.

No sooner had I recast than my bait moved and I had slack. It could have been the current moving it, or it could have been a fish. I had felt nothing but knew from experience that a bass could pick up a bait and give no warning pull, so I carefully took up the slack and felt the line. My heart was pounding as I willed a fish to be there, but the bait settled and I felt nothing else. Fifteen minutes later I noticed a slow drag, as if a piece of weed had drifted on to the line. But there was no drifting weed, and this was just a little too fast an increase in pressure. I didn't think about this, but somehow my mind decided that it had to be a fish and I struck hard, moving back and striking again. A good bass was on the other end and it splashed noisily in its surprise, then pulled hard as I held it. I struggled to loosen the clutch one turn, which would allow a fish over 4lb or so to take line, and the clutch buzzed as this fish made a rush for the horizon. After several yards of line had been pulled out, it surfaced and splashed again and I held it with a finger on the spool. Then I pumped the fish back slowly to my platform and threw the net into the water in readiness. Once near the shore, the bass swam strongly to the left, taking out more line and going over a rock which was now submerged, but which in the past had cost me several fish. I bent the rod sideways, enjoying the rounded shape and the pull of the fish, which kicked and seemed determined to stay there, but eventually it gave in and came back towards me. I pulled it to the net and then the bass decided to go again so I let it have another run. It is difficult for anyone to let a good fish go away, but you have to if you want to land it. The next time the fish was tired and did not have the strength to stop me pulling it over the net. This was a better fish, about 5lb, and since I had promised my mother a fish I carefully hit it hard over the eyes to kill it. The sack that I carry for the purpose was taken out and the fish wrapped up. I hastily tightened the clutch on the reel, rebaited and cast out again.

Half an hour later I knew that I would have to move after the next cast. Experience had shown that the bigger fish often came as the water rose over the ledge I stood on, when I would be fishing in about five feet of water. So this time when I rebaited I put the spare bait into the cool-box, put that into my rucksack and tied my bass on top of that. Putting the rucksack on my back, I was ready to fish on till the last minute in case of a late fish. I cast out, this time with water over my feet and the net partly submerged.

As I was wondering whether I would get wet going back, I suddenly realised that the line was slack, hanging into the water, and moving to the left in the current. My heart pounded and I took up the slack – definitely a fish there – and more slack. I could see the fish was swimming in to the left as the line was moving fast in that direction; it would be over that rock now. I took up the slack and even more slack came. The fish was even closer. 'It must be almost close enough to touch with the rod top,' I thought. I needed to keep still in case my presence spooked the fish. Then the line began to tighten and I struck hard, also aware that the clutch needed to be loosened rapidly. Good thing I did loosen it since this fish went off like a rocket; it was obviously a good one. I knew I had hooked it since the fish was close on a tight line and I had really belted it, so I loosened the clutch more and let the bass run. I wanted to net this fish first go since I was already worried about the incoming tide.

The battle was fought about thirty yards out and when the bass surfaced I could see it was quite a good one. I brought it back towards me and struggled in the water to lift my net out from under the weed that had washed over it. The bass meanwhile seemed to gain strength and swam off to the left. I put the net handle over my shoulder and set about getting the line back on the reel. This time I made no mistake and netted the fish neatly. It was a lovely fish and I retreated back over the ledge to drier land. This fish was a good seven pounds, but not eight. I was quite sure of this, since once I have caught a few fish in the season I am usually right to about 4oz with fish between 4 and 10lb. This fish was a fine prize and as I bent to unhook it I saw its eye move round, seemingly to look at my hand. I decided then that I would let it go; it had rewarded my patience, and I had enjoyed the morning. I would reward it in turn, so I carefully released it from the hook and placed it back in the water. It was slow to move off, as bigger fish usually are, but then it started trying to flap its tail and, when I released it, as it started to fall sideways it reacted suddenly and with a vigorous shake of its tail it swam off across the reef.

Gratefully, with that feeling of perfect satisfaction, I walked back up the steep path to the car. Two marvellous hours in a beautiful place, and three bass caught. I had lost no tackle, not that this was important, but it emphasised the suitability of my rig for this type of ground. I had noticed a fray in the line after the last fish, so I would need to examine it later, and I could now discard the hook which would start to rust. What a marvellous start to the day; breakfast would be sweeter this morning.

The fish I had kept at just over 5lb contained two shore crabs, and also two wrasse pieces that I had thrown back after rebaiting;

they were easily recognisable. The bass had obviously been swimming round there for a while, at least long enough to find three food items.

This had been a good, but not outstanding session. A really good morning would include an eight- or nine-pounder, or perhaps five or more good fish. Even though I have not caught a double-figure fish from that ledge, it remains my favourite place.

Legering at close range over shallow rocks is most exciting and rewarding bassing. A light rod can be used, usually with a line of 12–18lb, and leads will be ½oz–2oz. Casts of no more than thirty yards are usually sufficient and every little movement of the bait can be felt.

It is under these conditions that you discover just how gentle and fussy bass can sometimes be. The first time you detect the gentle pluck followed by a few inches of slack line (which you are tempted to believe is caused by a crab or blenny) and then a slow gentle drag, like a small fragment of weed on the line, you do nothing; and then you experience a slight slackening as the bass drops the bait. As you come to realise that it is a fish picking up your bait, you try for the first time to strike at the slow drag and in amazement discover you have hooked a fish, perhaps a good one of 7, 8 or 9lb. Never again do you worry about distance, or expect bass to bite hard. You become so keyed up, feeling for every little movement, that legering for bass is an immensely exciting business – you begin to realise that often it is the biggest fish that are the most gentle takers.

Gentle bites are most likely in shallower water, when the sea is calm, and where the current is weak. It is important to not let the bass feel resistance. You must give slack immediately after a bite indication to give the fish time to take the bait. If there is no current at all you can either freeline or use a tiny lead of ¼–½oz leaving a bow of slack line hanging in the water. Bites tend to be either a quick fall of the line or a twitching, followed by the line straightening out. You need to strike as the line straightens under these conditions. There are some occasions, indeed some places, where I am sure that any lead at all on the line will stop you catching bass. It is therefore important to expect bass to be very finicky sometimes, and to fish accordingly.

Above all, consider what your fish is doing: it is hunting for food. You are also a hunter, and you must never forget that a watery drama is enacted every time you get a bite. An animal that has a strong instinct for survival is trying to eat your bait. Give it every chance to do so, without alarming it, then spring the trap quickly and set the hook.

Legering on rocky shores can be summed up simply. You decide to try a rocky area; you choose a reasonable time and weather; you use a good, big bait and the least lead you can; you place the bait out where it will interest feeding fish; you do your best to avoid scaring the fish; you hold the rod and feel for bites. Often you will be unsuccessful, but once you learn to recognise the bites bass give, all you need to experience is one bite to know that you have fitted in a piece of the jigsaw. Note the time of tide, weather, etc., and write it all down in a diary. Gradually the bites you get and the fish you catch (or see others catch) will give you the knowledge you need to be successful on that patch. As a rock bass angler, you will never stop learning.

6

Fishing Deeper Water and Other Methods

. . . the big bass [14 pounds 2 ounces] slammed into the bait in over 100 feet of water.

Angler's Mail, 18 October 1986

AV While bass generally feed in shallow water they are also frequently taken from boats and good catches are made by bottom fishing in deep water. I have personal knowledge of decent bass taken from water many fathoms deep by bottom fishing. Several of these fish were over the magic 10lb in weight and were boated by anglers fishing in the Solent and to the east of the Isle of Wight; they were caught on squid and mackerel. Some were taken from wrecks and one was taken on a bait fished with an attractor spoon above it. The water over these marks was from 6 to 20 fathoms deep, so it can be seen that bass are adaptable animals willing to feed in a variety of places other than the ones they are usually associated with – namely, surf beaches, shallow rocks, estuaries, offshore sandbanks and reefs. A significant observation is that a high proportion of these deeper water bass are big ones. A friend of mine, Ross Staplehurst,* who is an expert boat fisherman from the Isle of Wight, has taken several accidental bass from his boat and their weights were usually about 7–8lb, with a couple weighing 10lb.

In the last fifteen years pressure on bass populations has been relentless. Commercial fishing often takes the form of gill-netting but some 'professional anglers' target inshore wrecks, using lures occasionally but more often using livebait, usually sandeels. These wreck-caught bass tend to be of good size.

---

* Ross, incidentally, must be the only man ever to have a shark jump into his boat. The 360lb thresher was fifteen feet long.

119

These examples of boat fishing make the point that bass are to be found on the bottom in some deeper water situations. In some places – rather few and far between – they can also regularly be caught in deeper water by fishing from the shore. The usual venues are rocky headlands, where there are also likely to be impressive tide races. Bass are caught by spinning in these tide races and it seems that often they are found rather deep down. In some of these places bottom fishing is also possible, although with the strong currents it may only be possible to fish on the seabed for a short part of the tide.

My own experience of deeper water bassing is mainly from the Menai Straits in North Wales. This stretch of water is ideal for bass for several reasons. There is a rough bottom in most places, and there is a very strong current – conditions which seem to suit large bass very well. The area is sheltered, so wave action is virtually non-existent and, consequently, there is an impressive growth of weed and a lot of shelter for bass food.

I have caught many bass in the Menai Straits area and from Anglesey, particularly from the area of the straits called the Swellies, between the two bridges. A lot of the time I was legering into several fathoms of water. The bait is invariably edible crab, since the fish

An 11¾lb bass taken on soft crab, from Anglesey.

Alan with four cracking bass (10lb 8oz, 7lb 6oz, 6lb 11oz, 6lb 5oz), from the deep, powerful flow of the Menai Straits.

there take it better than anything else. Because of the rough nature of the ground and the strong currents, leads of 3–6oz and a line of 28lb with hook and lead links of 23lb are needed. Not pretty fishing, but it is a specialised business, and the quarry are big fish. A lot of tackle is lost but I have had catches of 25lb+ consisting of three or four fish only. The average size of the fish can be as much as 8lb.

Occasionally the only fish that appear to be present are very big ones. During 1980 Phil Williams and I fished the Menai Straits for a week during July. During the first three days there were few bites and the only bass was a fish of 7½lb to Phil. Under these circumstances, it is important not to lose heart and never to forget that the fish can turn up any day. It is vital to keep putting out good, big baits.

On the fourth day things began slowly. I had a bite soon after low water, but it was nearly two hours later when Phil took the first fish. I had moved along the beach to try a spot where, in previous years, I had taken bass of 9lb and 10lb and I was looking in Phil's direction when I saw him strike into what was obviously a very good fish. I watched with interest, wondering whether he was attached to a bass or a conger. If it was a conger I would stay put, but if it was a bass I would rejoin Phil at our original spot, where we knew from experience that big fish came late in the tide. I was very excited when I saw that the fish was certainly not a conger.

I rushed along the beach to see the magnificent bass that Phil had just beached. He weighed it and the balance went down to 10½lb. With trembling fingers I baited up a large soft edible crab and cast out. I felt a slight twitch on the line and gave some slack; the line was taken up and a pull began to develop. I struck and the rod bent right over as line was taken against the clutch. This fish pulled harder than any bass I had yet caught and, when it eventually lay beaten at the edge of the ledge, it looked enormous. Phil lifted it ashore and we weighed it swiftly: 12¼lb. Two double-figure bass in fifteen minutes – fantastic!

There were no more bites nor fish that day. On the remaining four days we fished in the Swellies and at Beaumaris from Gallows Point, but the only other bass was a fish of 4½lb to my rod. In terms of numbers of bass caught, this was quite easily my worst week in the straits, but of course no one complains when one of the fish caught is a twelve-pounder and two out of the four fish caught are doubles.

In deeper water, whether or not the current is really belting along, bass definitely feed more confidently than in shallow water. However, in such circumstances bite detection can be difficult and, as in shallow water, the angler must always hold the rod to be consistently successful. The Menai Straits locals usually fish using a rod rest, as I did myself years ago, but the idea that a bass will take a bait and virtually hook itself is wrong. It is difficult to overemphasise that many big fish are missed when a rod rest is used. Fifteen years ago more people fished there from the shore, there were more bass and some of those fish were caught on rods left in rod rests. Now there are fewer bass but they are a lot bigger, and these big bass are not so easy to catch. My two biggest bass from the area, both twelve-pounders, were hooked after very gentle takes; I am sure I would have ignored the rod tip movement had the rod been on a rest.

Despite the tremendous longshore flow, it is also possible to take fish from the Menai Straits by spinning. This was revealed by Tony Shepherdson in a letter to Mike, which is quoted practically word for word:

I fished Hell's Mouth on the Lleyn Peninsula and Dinas Dinlle for a week in May [1984], but both beaches are very heavily fished and I did well to get what I did (nine fish to 4½lb). I fished your patch in Easter without result by your methods, and attributed my lack of fish to the early season plus inexperience. I found it very interesting and will be back next Easter for sure when I hope to meet you.

While in North Wales, I took plugs and spinning rod down to the Menai Straits between the two bridges crossing the straits – the famous Swellies – at which point the 8-knot tide is concentrated into a series of rapids and overfalls, but along the shoreline it is very calm. At low water the foreshore is very rocky with a series of little groynes, lagoons and channels and offers a very rich, shallow feeding ground to bring in the bass.

I arrived on the last hour of the ebb and passed the next two hours by spinning a Toby in the slack between the island and my shore. The tide was making slowly and it would obviously be another three hours before it reached the shallow, rocky lagoons.

I had a sleep after reconnoitring the area which I eventually intended to fish. It was a late evening tide and when I woke up there was about an hour of light left; by this time, the high foreshore was flooding nicely. Wading rocky ground on the edge of dusk is a little tricky, but I managed to work my way out slowly to about mid-thigh depth before I began to work the plug. As the tips of the rocky scars were uncovered, it was still possible to visualise the channels and, again, as I found in Dorset, I was amazed at the ease with which I could fish through such snaggy ground without getting fast.

I cast for about forty minutes and then moved down the shore to fish a large lagoon bounded on the seaward side by a long stone groyne. I dropped the plug about thirty yards out between two rocky outcrops and wound about two turns when something slammed into the plug with unbelievable force, wrenching the rod top right down to the water surface. It took me completely by surprise. The clutch was set very lightly and by the time I had collected my wits the fish had shot about twenty yards diagonally, round the back of the rocks, and I was snagged. Years of pulling chub out from under willow bushes should have prepared me for hanging on grimly, but everything happened so quickly! I decided it wasn't worth the risk of wading waist-deep out to the rocks on the edge of dusk, so I pulled for a break. (Can you hear me sobbing now, Mike?)

Though I never saw the fish, it was the biggest bass I've ever hooked. I fish a 10½-foot carbon rod which is a very powerful fish-stopper, and I've had enough double-figure pike to know what a good fish feels like, but I've never had a fish before which slammed into a bait so hard and fast. We had to go home next day, but when I visit North Wales again I shall haunt the rocky shore along the straits on every tide. I hooked the fish on a large, gold-tinted, jointed Rebel.

After reading Tony's letter it struck me that he was probably a little foolhardy. I have fished the Swellies for fifteen years and I know just how dangerous it would be to fall in, so I must add that I strongly advise anglers to stay on the edge rather than wade. I certainly wouldn't wade, and I know the area very well indeed. In any case, in most places it would be pointless to wade since the shore is deeply shelving and the fish come very close in.

Over the years my friends and I have spent many hours spinning in the straits with Tobys and other spoons, but although we have caught many mackerel, with some pollack and coalfish, we have taken only a few bass. Legering has always seemed a more productive method. However, in the light of Mike's experience and Tony's comments, it seems that plugs could be a lot more effective, and I will be using them in the future.

ML Other deep water marks certainly respond to spinning tactics. In the Portland race off Dorset, the commercial methods of bassing have evolved quite rapidly due to the pressures of supply, demand and expediency. When the fishermen first began to catch bass in the deep, fast water, they used large, single-jointed Rapala plugs, usually tethered to a suitably heavy lead. This was very effective fished on the drift in the fierce tidal currents. Presumably the bass hooked themselves and, on the heavy gear, were winched up and unhooked. Unhooking must have presented considerable problems. Imagine a wet, slippy deck heaving over a rough sea and a lively bass of 13 or 14lb lashing about with three big, sharp trebles flapping from its jaw. Not a pretty thought.

The second development was an attempt to improve on the artificial bait. Many of the bass caught had been feeding on mackerel and, since the latter were easy to feather up on site, it was only natural to use them for bait. The method was to employ a very large treble on a simple paternoster. One point of the hook was inserted through the nostril of the mackerel and it was lowered down to the bass, which engulfed it and hooked itself. Apparently at slack tide the fish were generally deep down and, as the tide ran more strongly they could be caught nearer and nearer the surface. When mackerel were in short supply or to make sure that fishing could commence at once, other small fish were used as bait with good effect. The most recent development, presumably following on the declining abundance of mackerel, is to use sandeels as bait and it appears that these are as good as, or better than, any of the above-mentioned tactics.

Talking of sandeels recalls the fishery to the west of the Isle of Wight where sandeel is and, as far as I know, always has been the staple bait. The interesting feature of the method used in these deep waters is the fact that each fisherman holds two rods, one in either hand. The idea is that when a bass takes the sandeel on one rod it is hooked but not reeled in. Apparently the presence of a fish swerving and flashing on the first rod is liable to attract a customer to the second bait much more often than would otherwise be the case.

Of course, sandeel has been used as a prime bass bait for many, many years. In the narrow mouth of Poole Harbour, reasonably light tackle weighted with an ounce or two of pierced bullet has been the standard tactic for a long time. The flotilla of small boats is visible on any summer day, drifting through the harbour mouth with every angler dangling a sandeel into the deep, grey-blue water. Pouting are also commonly used as bait in this situation. Similar tactics are effectively used by land-based anglers fishing from the lifting bridge in Poole Harbour itself, and fish of 12 or 13lb have been caught in this way, although many of them were much smaller.

Tide races like those described are rarely as accessible as the strong flows which pass under bridges. Often the race will be a good deal further offshore and, quite likely, well beyond normal casting distance. At St Aldhelm's Head, Dorset, there is a terrific tide race which is easily visible from the rocks. Standing beneath the massive and awe-inspiring cliff and casting from a boulder vantage point with a heavy Toby, it is just about possible to reach

A 2lb codling with an 8½lb bass. In deeper water they can be caught together in summer when bait fishing.

the edge of the white water. Between the angler and the race is a fast-flowing 'salt river' with, here and there, a gigantic submerged boulder. Every so often, out in the main flow, the mackerel will spray from the sea, hustled from beneath by some fast-swimming predator. On a good evening the Toby will be seized by mackerel and bass alike, but always one has the feeling that the casts are a good fifty yards short of the real hot spot.

The Portland race itself has been fished from the shore for many years. Again it is well offshore, but the methods used by local anglers may have a much wider application all around our south and west coasts. The general idea is to take advantage of long casting, wind and currents to carry the lure to where the fish are, certainly way beyond the casting capacity of standard spinning tackle. The basic idea is to employ a powerful beach-casting rod with a lead of about 4oz in the float. To prevent the tackle sinking irretrievably to the seabed, a hefty sliding float capable of supporting lead and lure is fitted to the line. The lure itself is the good old Redgill. Using this gear, from a suitable vantage point, it is possible to get the lure well offshore – though there cannot be too many spots which are ideally suited. The bass presumably have to hook themselves on the Redgill, which trails with its tail frantically wagging as the water rushes by. It must be impossible to strike effectively at such long range, but there seems no doubt of the effectiveness of this specialised method.

In South Wales, in rather shallower water, anglers fishing power station outfalls have devised a similar method, incorporating plastic eels, to catch their bass. To get the eel out to the fish they have developed a modification of the coarse fisherman's old-fashioned wooden leger, which gave casting weight without dragging the gear to the bottom. Instead of the rather tricky wood-carving exercise, they make use of modern technology by filling a plastic Jif lemon with candle grease. I shall repeat the description given to me by a man who has caught many bass by this method, Bob Spurgeon:

Since the bass were first noticed in the power-station outfalls many years ago, the technique for catching them has developed slowly, until now the use of a Jif is universal. Most anglers today just copy the method, which is of course very simple, but whoever devised it is a genius.

The problem is how to fish a lure at a distance of a hundred yards, over a rough bottom with, perhaps, only two feet of water above horrific snags. The solution is to use a floating weight and a very light lure. The set-up is as follows:

In its most developed form, the Jif is filled with candle wax and weighs about 2½oz. I fish it on a three-way swivel, but most people use it straight through. The normal lure is a 112mm Redgill sandeel. I preferred the original 'boxed' version but now that the 'commercial' has come to dominate the market they are the

4ft

Redgill

Wax-filled 'Jif'

Wax-filled Jif lemon rig for fishing an eel at long distance in a strong flow of water.

cheapest and usually the only available eels. Personally, I don't like this eel because it tends to spin in the water. I much prefer the, more expensive, 115mm Rascal. Eddystone eels also work well. I have confidence in the silver belly/blue back and no one has ever consistently outfished me using anything else.

My line is 15lb BS. I would like to fish with lighter lines, but overruns or bale-arm trouble which stop the Jif in mid-flight will easily part them. With the 15lb line it is rare to lose any gear.

The trace length is critical. Many anglers are inclined to use a trace that is too short. The exact length must be varied to suit the conditions. The use of a weight on the trace is a matter for experiment too; most anglers prefer to use a heavy swivel to sink the Redgill, and again its position is critical – attach it in the wrong place and the casting dynamics are all wrong, causing the trace to cartwheel through the air. With a lot of anglers fishing the best arrangement of trace length, etc., will soon become obvious. Usually four feet without added weight will work.

Normally I am fishing across streams of hot water from the power station. In these situations the most effective technique is not to reel in at all, but to let the lure 'swim' across the current. When the bass are in the area they seem unable to resist a 'sandeel' swimming, almost stationary in the current, in this way. Some years ago I watched a shoal of brit under the pier at Yarmouth, Isle of Wight. They were swimming against the tide but making no headway. A school of bass was beneath them and one rose up, took a brit and returned to its level without the shoal of bait-fish moving at all. If it proves possible to fish the lure in this manner I always try to do it, otherwise I retrieve as slowly as I can.

Alan tells me that he has only once tried fishing the outfalls at Aberthaw with the Jif lemon technique. On that occasion he fished with Martin Giddy, and they used spinning rods with 8lb line and leaders of 15lb line. Using this tackle, they easily outcast a number of other anglers fishing with heavier tackle, and took about a dozen small bass each – far more than anyone else. Delta eels proved a lot better than Redgills. All Alan's and Martin's bass were returned but, very sadly, other anglers were keeping some. How can we get through to these short-sighted people?

It is interesting to note that at Aberthaw, where the Jif was developed, only small bass are taken by this method (usually fish of less than 2lb). However, there are big fish to be taken by fishing on the bottom, in the deeper water. The Welsh record bass from the shore, a magnificent fish of 16lb 15½oz, was taken here on legered peeler shore crab by Don Cook in July 1980. Other very big bass have been taken here and Don has seen a bigger bass than his record while boat fishing near the ledges.

Lures other than Redgills can also be effective in deep water situations. Light plugs, for example, may be trolled from a powered dinghy to take near-surface fish, but this is a method of which I have little experience. Ken Mew, who has caught many large bass on Rapala plugs in the Poole Bay area, tells me that the wind can make it very difficult to fish with these lures. To overcome wind drag on the line, Ken adds a small pierced bullet, stopped by a 'quick-release' bristle about fifteen or twenty yards ahead of the plug (usually a J9 floating Rapala). This weight sinks the line and ensures that the lure fishes more effectively. Ken has landed a number of 11 and 12lb fish on trolled plugs as well as a quantity of good sea trout, so he is a man well worth listening to.

Other specialised boat-fishing methods for bass are essentially outside the scope of this book, but we feel it necessary to mention them.

Trolling plastic eels (Redgills, Eddystones, etc.) over offshore reefs or in other areas frequented by bass is a very effective method. Using suitably light tackle, this method can be very exciting, but where the method is used over the Eddystone many of the 'professional anglers' employ extremely heavy line and large weights. The British record bass of 18lb 6oz was taken here in this fashion.

Off the Essex coast and elsewhere, over clean bottoms, uptide fishing, using wired leads and various baits, produces many bass. Essentially, a large bow is left in the line and a fish lifting a bait dislodges the weight, whereupon water pressure on the line pulls the hook into the fish's mouth. Off Essex, where many big bass are taken, a favourite bait is ragworm.

What general conclusions can be drawn from these accounts? It seems possible that the really big fish are most likely to come from locations like the Menai Straits, Portland, or the deep water off the Isle of Wight. It is difficult to prove the point, and few anglers are willing to try fishing in conditions which are so difficult, where the lead jams in the bottom, the rod bends over and you try to detect and react to bites which are not always very obvious. We suggest, however, that you have a go in this type of situation, since the bass do feed more confidently than when they are over shallow rock, even though there are other difficulties. To illustrate the point about the large size of fish, during one holiday week of angling in just such a situation, Alan caught three bass of over 10lb in deep water from the shore, and during another week two bass of 11¾lb and 12¾lb. So, if you have the patience and the determination and you know such a situation, with a fast current and deep water over a rough bottom, that may be where you find your fish of a lifetime.

Since 1990 I have had little opportunity to fish in North Wales and my chances to use spinning techniques to catch bass in the Menai Straits have been limited. However, I have been in touch with dedicated lure anglers in the area and it is clear from the excellent catches made by Steve Butler and Mike Hughes that big bass can regularly be caught by spinning from the shore in this unusual venue where fast tide rips and deep water separate Anglesey from the mainland.

7
Sandy Beaches

In the Gower peninsula . . . the local experts have evolved another method . . . wading in and casting out on the flood tide into the shallow sandy bays, where there are often a good many bass in the summer months.
F. D. Holcombe, *Modern Sea Angling*, 1921

Traditionally a good deal of bass fishing has involved casting into classic storm-beach surfs. So much has been written about the huge catches of bass from the great Irish surf strands, such as Stradbally and Inch, and the Welsh beaches at Freshwater West, Cefn-Sidan and Dinas Dinlle, that anglers can be forgiven if they think that this is the only worthwhile bass fishing.

Certainly these beaches are beautiful and one is so easily affected by an awareness of the power of the elements as the wind and water rush towards you. Also, the strands are often remote in a lovely desolate way. You can easily forget the trials and frustrations of working life; the mortgage payments and electricity bills are never further away than when you stand alone on a vast surf beach, waiting for a shoal of bass to sweep down the strand to your bait.

What is true, but rarely mentioned, is that when your catches come from such beaches they are likely to be smallish fish. Years ago the Welsh and Irish beaches regularly produced numbers of quality fish, but nowadays you are less likely to catch a lot of good sized bass from the surf. However, such is the attraction of these beaches that many anglers feel there is nothing to beat catching a bass from the pounding surf.

AV Sandy beaches come in all sizes and are found in a variety of situations. Those facing the prevailing winds, with a westerly or southerly aspect, are usually very exposed and thus present harsh conditions for would-be inhabitants, since heavy surf often shifts and stirs up the seabed. Fine particles are swept away, so these beaches tend to have clean and fairly coarse sand, often backed by a shingly, pebbly foreshore. Unstable sand is unsuitable as a habitat for many sea creatures; lugworms, for example, need relatively undisturbed sediment in which to burrow and few are to be found on very exposed shores.

Some animals, however, are capable of surviving the turmoil of surf and sand – molluscs such as razorfish live safely in deep burrows at or below the low water mark, while others, such as queen cockles, with thick, strong shells, are adapted to being tumbled about when they are uprooted by fierce wave action. There may be sandeels sheltering in the sand at night, and also masked crabs and small swimming crabs, along with a few common shore crabs and small white sandhoppers. So these beaches do hold a larder stocked with bass food, but it is unlikely to be a rich harvest for the marauding fish unless there is a good surf rolling in to disturb the sand.

There will be exceptions, of course – for instance, when sandeels are swimming close inshore when conditions are calm and the weather sunny, or when small food animals are washed on to the beach from a neighbouring estuary by a river in spate. However, exposed sandy beaches, as a rule, fish best when the weather drives the white horses on to the shore.

Beaches sheltered by an offshore reef or by an arm of land or because they face east or north will be at least partly sheltered and sections of the beach are likely to be fairly stable. The stable area will probably be dotted with the little sand-piles of lugworms and beneath the surface many more shellfish and crabs will be present. Sea conditions on these beaches are calmer and they carry a surf only when the wind blows directly onshore. Under such an onshore blow, there may be a lot of white water, but rarely will it be as spectacular as the tables of surf rushing on to an Atlantic storm beach. Generally, partly sheltered beaches will be less productive for bass than the real storm beaches.

Really sheltered beaches are found inside bays, natural harbours and estuaries. They are also present in places like the Solent, where there is not enough 'fetch' for the wind to build up large waves. The sediment on these shores is finer and will often be muddy. An enormous variety of worms, molluscs and crustaceans is found on such beaches and they are the favourite bait-gathering grounds for anglers, but they are rarely much good for catching bass.

Muddy shores are likely to be rather inhospitable in a rough sea. The visibility quickly falls to zero, as mud is whipped into suspension and fish cannot use sight as a means of finding food. One sheltered beach (the Lafan sands near Bangor, North Wales) which I fished successfully for good-sized bass over a number of years produced well when the sea was calm and the wind offshore, but, with any hint of an onshore blow to build up significant waves, the fishing was useless as the shallow water quickly became turbid with suspended silt.

It is well known that bass are attracted to rocky patches and, possibly, to freshwater inflows along an otherwise featureless sandy beach. I have found this to be true, both on sheltered and exposed shores. (However, peat-stained water running off high ground after heavy rain – as occurs in North Wales and Eire – will put fish off rather than attract them.) Gullies also seem to attract fish and it is probable that *any* unusual feature on an otherwise smooth, flat strand will hold bass, so it is always worth choosing a fishing position within reach of such features.

Another 'well-known fact' is that low water and early flood are good times to fish, with another 'prime time' coming at high water. The truth is that bass may turn up at any state of tide. But on spring tides over gently sloping beaches the sea sweeps quickly in and out at mid-tide, which means that frequent moves and recasting will be necessary, particularly in regions such as South Wales, where the tidal range is very large.

Anglers have known for many years that when bass are feeding over sandy beaches, in conditions which produce a steady, regular pattern of breaking waves, the feeding fish become concentrated in a fairly narrow band running parallel to the sea's edge. When the sea is rough, this band may be beyond casting range, but in a moderate surf it can be very close to the angler, especially if he is wading. On most such occasions a cast of from fifty to eighty yards will be plenty to cover the fish. When the feeding distance has been found, it is necessary to fish at the same range every time until contact is lost, when the search must begin again.

Sometimes the fish will be very close in and I shall never forget when once fishing Fermoyle Strand in Brandon Bay, Co. Kerry. I was wading out beyond a friend and his cast fell short, barely passing me and about fifty yards to the right. As I stood in water up to my knees, I was treated to the sight of him striking into and playing a good-sized bass back to the beach. The fish was hooked no more than fifty yards from dry sand and in only two feet of water. The bass, a nine-pounder, which took a clam, was the only fish of the session.

During another Irish summer holiday, I recall fishing a daytime tide on a small sandy beach near Brandon village. The weather was sunny and quite calm, with only a single wave turning over at the edge of the sea. Casting sixty yards, neither I nor my two companions caught a bass (although I had a mackerel). However, by shortening our casts to the area just behind the breaking wave, about twenty yards out, we caught half a dozen bass averaging about 4lb. All the fish took mackerel strips.

One advantage of fishing over a sandy or shingly bottom is that relatively fine line can be used with little risk of losing tackle on snags. Some anglers prefer to use a fine line with a shock leader. This has the (dubious) advantage of greater casting potential and the real advantage of reduced water pressure on the line, which means that lighter leads can be used. There are one or two circumstances in which fine lines cause problems. If drifting weed is encountered it will accumulate on the line and may make it impossible to retrieve without breakage. Also, weed always piles up on the leader knot, which may then jam in the tip ring. Lastly, when fishing from shingle beaches the shifting pebbles can trap or pinch the line, causing loss of tackle.

An alternative to the shock leader is to use a line of 15–18lb BS all through and a lead of 2 or 3oz, employing a forgiving casting style. I think that I am in a minority but this is my choice. Perhaps it is a minority of two, because Mike says he does exactly the same.

Whatever distance one casts, it pays to move along the beach with the drift so that the line enters the water at right angles. If breakaway or fixed-wire leads are used it is unlikely that the tackle will shift – unless it is moved by a fish or by a very heavy surf. Normal leads will often slide or roll along and it will be necessary to follow them along the shore and maintain a tight line to avoid the tackle being quickly swept inshore.

The rod must be held at all times, but there is a choice of methods. My own preference when there is little or no drifting weed is to point the rod straight down the line, holding the line between finger and thumb. If, however, weed fragments are

134

An 8½lb bass taken on a mackerel head from a sandy beach.

washing in along the tide-line, or when waves pull at the line, it is necessary to keep the rod point up.

Terminal tackle should be a fixed or running paternoster. Bass generally take quickly in turbulent conditions, so early bite detection and an immediate strike are then the order of the day. Fortunately, the bites are usually quite noticeable: a strong pull or hard knocks are common and so is sudden slackening of the line. All bites must be struck at once – tactics quite different from those used over rocky ground. However, if an unwired lead is used and if sea conditions are heavy, you will need to remind yourself that there is a great deal of background movement to get used to before you strike wildly at every slight sensation. This is exaggerated by the continuous movement of shifting sand underfoot, caused by retreating waves, which means that you are continually having to adjust your own position as you wait for bites.

Baits used for surf fishing, whether they are worms, razorfish, sandeels or fish strips, should be quite large and well threaded on or securely fixed to the hook. Several decent-sized lugworms, or a whole razorfish foot, or even two, are about right. Hooks can be smaller than those used over rocks since the bait is less bulky than a typical rock-fished bait. Different anglers have different preferences, ranging from size 1/0 to 5/0, but a 3/0 is a fair compromise.

Landing fish on a gently sloping sandy beach is – or should be – very straightforward. Bass of any size should never be horsed in, but they can be beached if you regain line, lift the rod and move backwards with each advancing wave. A tight line is essential because, when striking a fish at any distance, there is never any guarantee that it is hooked beyond the barb and, if slack line is given, the point may fall out. At the other extreme it is a grave mistake to try to pull a fish through the undertow. If it is played with patience, the fish will eventually become grounded and the trick is then to pick it up quickly before the next wave rescues it – or soaks you to the skin. A big fish will ground itself in deeper water than a small one and it is often a good idea for a companion to cut off its escape by getting behind it in case it comes off the hook. A gaff or net is rarely essential in these circumstances.

The surf-beach angler needs to think about suitable clothing for his sport. Waders are almost a must and some anglers prefer chest waders to overcome the problem of waves rising or splashing over wader tops. If waterproof trousers are worn over thigh waders, then many of the larger waves may recede before the water finds its way up between boots and trousers. If strong rubber bands, for example strips of inner tube, are put around trouser bottoms, there is a good chance of remaining dry to the waist throughout a session. A waterproof jacket is also advisable, since splashes are inevitable and it only needs one big wave to soak clothing and spoil a session.

Because beach fishing for bass involves a lot of moving about to keep up with the tide, it pays to avoid taking a lot of equipment. It is best to carry everything in pockets or in a small haversack. If you establish a base camp further up the beach make sure it is high enough and that you remember exactly where it is when darkness falls. Nowhere is it easier to get lost than on a flat, sandy beach at night, and it will often pay to fish beaches at night because results are frequently better than in daytime.

Spinning into the surf over sand is probably rarely attempted in this country, although in the United States, with their tradition of lure fishing, anglers have plenty of success in catching their native fish by this method. Under suitable conditions (probably a slight or moderate surf) plugs, spoons or silicone rubber eels will undoubtedly be effective. My own experience of such tactics is limited and the only occasion when I saw such methods used successfully was during a breezy, overcast afternoon fishing at Llandwyn Island on the Isle of Anglesey. Three of us had been spinning from the rocky headland for mackerel and bass, without success. A walk back to the car took us past a sandy beach where a single wave was breaking impressively on the shore. We all cast out several times, bouncing our Toby spoons back across the sandy bottom. Ivan was the only one to have any success and the only one using dark-coloured spoons. He landed two bass of about 4lb each, almost on successive casts, returning each one to the water. There was some sort of snag present and Ivan did lose one Toby before we packed up, but we were spinning over more or less clean sand and, for a short time at least, a shoal of bass was present and in feeding mood. Experience has shown that in such daytime conditions a legered bait might well have been ignored. If spinning were more often tried in the surf, then a lot more bass might be caught.

ML As Alan has said, the flat strands of south-west Ireland are renowned for their fabulous bass fishing. Dr Michael Kennedy, who has done much research on Irish bass, says that bass 'show a preference for mixed beaches of sand and rocks', but that they are commonly found on 'flat shelving beaches of gravelly sand fronting the open sea'. Flat areas of muddy sand are also hunted by foraging bass as the tide floods. Michael Kennedy gives a graphic description of the situation on Irish sandy-mud flats: 'As the tide rises, they swim in over the strand in search of food, as soon as it is covered up by a foot or two of water.' If the water is coloured the bass will 'nose about' along the edge of the strand, 'their waving tails sometimes breaking the surface'. A little later the same author comments that an onshore wind 'sends bass into the surf along the shelving beaches, especially on the first of the flood, . . . they will often be *very* close inshore'. He also comments that 'when there is very little surf they will frequently be twenty to fifty or more yards out' on the same beaches.

So here we have an expert marine biologist and a very experienced bass angler pointing out that even on shallow, sandy and gravelly beaches the fish are little more than twenty yards out when there is a bit of surf. My own experience is in total agreement. On one occasion I recall fishing a sandy cove at Gara Rock in South Devon. The beach consisted of gritty orange-yellow sand and sloped quite steeply. I knew that bass were present along the beach because I had seen them on a number of occasions. On the day in question the sea was calm and clear, with only a light groundswell turning lazily over almost at the water's edge. There was perhaps two yards of turbid, sandy water just where the waves were breaking, while, beyond, every pebble and grain of sand was clearly visible.

It would have been quite difficult to fish from the beach at such short range (I guessed that any bass present would be patrolling the breaking waves) so I settled for a vantage point on the steep rock-face flanking the east side of the cove. Perched well above the sea and about fifteen yards seaward of the mini-surf, I could flick a bait (I had lugworm and one or two dead sandeels) in towards the beach. The tackle consisted of a half-ounce running bomb and a three-foot trace. Since snags were non-existent, the line on my fixed spool reel was only 6lb BS and the rod was a light 10-foot carp rod. The only fish I caught were bass. All of them were small, with the best only a couple of pounds, and the only bites I could get came right in the water's edge.

Along the golden beaches of Bournemouth bay and the superb strands of Studland, Swanage and Weymouth there are often plenty of school bass to be caught with just a few larger specimens to keep you on your toes. In calm conditions the fish will sometimes be hard to come by and after-dark fishing may be the only way to catch any number. Of course, when fishing at night there will usually be any amount of pouting and poor cod to rattle away at the rod top, but when there is coloured water as the result of an onshore blow it is quite a different story. Even in daylight under these conditions, worm and fish baits presented close in are likely to be snapped up by bass. Simple light leger or paternoster tackle is usually adequate and it may often be possible to pick out any larger fish present by using bigger baits such as mackerel fillets, small freshwater eels or sandeels, but it is surprising just how large a bait a 1½lb schooly will gollop down.

The major problem on some of these sandy south-coast beaches is the presence of the holidaymakers. In summer the air will reek of sun tan lotion and, although bass don't seem to mind this and may be quite close inshore, it is definitely antisocial – and lacks a certain flavour of the great outdoors – to cast your bait between the paddlers, rubber boats and bikini-clad maidens. Try dusk, night or dawn to avoid the hassle and increase the chances of catching decent fish.

Conditions which bring the bass close in over sand present fantastic opportunities for fishing light but sensible tackle. It is possible to present any chosen bait on relatively fine line with the very minimum of weight, in the knowledge that even the largest bass can be played to a standstill, unhampered by lumps of lead.

At Swanage, Dorset, on the gently sloping sand of the sea front, I have caught quite a few bass on live or dead common eels and brook lampreys. Both baits were taken, close in, with all the eagerness shown by bass for worm, prawn, or any other of the more usual sea-angling baits.

As I have already suggested, because in calm conditions over sand bass feed so close inshore for much of the time there may be no need to add lead for casting. A decent-sized crab or fish bait, even a hefty ragworm, can easily be placed within range of feeding fish with no weight other than the hook. So why not fish like this all the time? Strong tidal currents will sweep a freelined bait back inshore very quickly. This may not be such a bad thing, if there are plenty of fish about, but it creates some problems if the bass are known to be only a little further out. Wind can also be difficult to contend with – 'bowing' in the unweighted line makes it very tricky to keep adequate contact with the bait.

The time to seriously consider freelining is when fish are known or anticipated to be close in, in calm conditions at slack water or during neap tides. The ideal situation for these tactics is along pebbly storm beaches such as the famous – or notorious – Chesil Bank in Dorset, and in little shingle-backed coves, of which there are many along the channel coast.

The best introduction to the method which I can give is to quote from Lloyd, writing in 1914. Although the example is so old, the method and its potential could not be described better. This excerpt refers to a steep, shelving, gravel beach six miles west of Sidmouth in Devon and he writes:

On the morning of 20 June 1914, and a very hot morning it was, I had tramped this stretch of shingle for several somewhat weary hours, trying in various ways, but all in vain, to lure a bass from the watery deep. The morning, as I have said, was hot; the shingle was loose and the 'going' consequently heavy.

Lloyd goes on to describe how he sat on the shingle for a breather and found a small, dead, smelly mackerel discarded by the fishermen, then he says: 'I hastily flung it away. It dropped not a yard out to sea . . . and then the miracle came to pass. A long, grey shadow slid into view, absorbed the mackerel . . . and vanished again.' He then describes how, by free-lining a slice of mackerel on a 5/0 hook, at high water, seldom more than three yards from the water's edge, he took a good many bass with the average weight over the year being about six pounds.

My own experience, in Dorset, suggests that this method is of general application and that it will work at any state of the tide and in flat-calm, gin-clear conditions. Of course, this is not to say that bass are always present on every beach and, there is no substitute for knowing the fishes' timetable for each stretch of shoreline.

On one gently shelving, fairly sheltered coarse-grit beach which I know, anglers walking along the shore at low water are likely to be surprised by a mighty swirl a few yards ahead of them as a big bass shoots away from the water's edge. If you are patient and sit down on the shingle (as Mr Lloyd did) it will not be too long before you notice one or more little groups of ripples within a few feet of the beach. Careful observation will show that these disturbances are caused by the upper lobes of bass tails, just touching or breaking the surface film.

It will soon be obvious that the fish are patrolling along the edge of the sea, head down and tail up, searching for food. Each bass will usually patrol back and forth along a thirty- or forty-yard beat, turning and returning at the end of every patrol. The thing to do is to pick your fish (assuming that there are more than one); cast your leadless bait into the path of the fish you have selected; leave the bale arm of the reel disengaged; hold the line gently between finger and thumb; and wait. The bass may now ignore your bait for several passes, but, with a bit of luck, eventually you will have a take. The takes which I have experienced invariably involved the fish gently picking up the bait, then swimming in a steady, purposeful manner out to sea. The problem now is when to strike? I generally give the fish plenty of time, allowing the line to run out freely for five or ten seconds before striking hard. Unfortunately, this has resulted in about 50 per cent of misses, but quite a few big fish landed. (Now I wait for the fish to stop and then to start running for a second time before I strike – the method is taxing on the heart but my experience suggests that fish are rarely missed when doing this.)

The number of missed runs can hardly be due to the fish having failed to get the bait in their mouths and is more likely to be caused by the difficulty of setting a large hook on light tackle. There are two obvious ways of solving the problem. First, make sure plenty of hook is exposed and hit the fish very hard – as hard as the tackle will allow. This definitely improves results. Springy Aberdeen hooks, although sharp and fine in the wire, may not be as good as they would appear to be. The second approach is to use small trebles on the same principles as a pike snap-tackle and strike quickly. I have not yet tried this but see no reason why it would not be very effective. The only problem might be the weed-collecting properties of one or more trebles.

With regard to baits, I have no evidence that what is on the hook makes much difference. In similar conditions I have seen fish take crab, ragworm, sandeel and squid. All the fish caught so far have been between five and nine pounds in weight, but smaller ones are present and larger ones have been lost.

The method works in darkness as well as in daylight and may, in fact, be better in the gloom. The major problem, of course, is that it is not possible to stalk fish at night because you cannot easily see them. There seem to be plenty of fish inshore after dark and I quote one example.

Terry Gledhill and I had spent an evening spinning for bass on a long, curving shingle beach near Chapman's Pool, Dorset. We had not had a sniff. As darkness fell we worked our way back along the beach for a final cast in the shallowest corner of the bay, near the rugged headland rocks. I changed to a tiny jointed black-and-silver J7 Rapala for my final effort. I cast into the black water and the plug was seized, first cast, two or three yards out with a powerful lunge; a heavy fish fought back and forth along the beach. When Terry lifted it out, we weighed it and, at $8\frac{1}{2}$lb, it was a real beauty. We each had a few more casts and then decided to try with bait. 4/0 hooks were tied directly to the spinning lines and baited with whole small calamari squid, hooked once through the pointed end.

The squid were lobbed a few feet out from the edge and then we sat back on the gravel to wait. Almost at once, Terry's line twitched and began to pour off the spool. He sat up from his reclining pose on the shingle and allowed the nylon to run out smoothly between his fingers. 'Give it plenty of time!' I said, having experienced a missed bite a couple of days earlier. Terry waited and waited and waited, and still the bass ran off with the bait. He brought over the bale arm and allowed the rod to curve to the pull of the fish before striking – the clutch buzzed briefly and the line fell slack. He had failed to connect with what would certainly have been our second big bass of the session.

There is little point in expanding further on margin-fishing, freelining methods for beach fishing, except to say that no bass angler should lack the confidence to try 'carp' tactics when they seem to be appropriate. There is no doubt that stealth and short casts are capable of producing very big bass and that baits such as whole squid, mackerel, pouting or wrasse could tempt real monsters from the water's edge for those with the right approach.

8
Estuaries

The size of estuary bass usually increases progressively towards the estuary mouth.

Michael Kennedy, *Salt Water Angling*, 1956

We have both caught bass in estuaries large and small and, whatever the reasons, it is certain that many bass are caught in brackish water. Bass, in common with eels, flounders and mullet, are sea fish which can tolerate changes in salinity and enter fresh water to feed there. Most of the fish we have caught in estuaries have been small, but a lot of big bass are caught in such situations and Alan was lucky enough once to take a fish of just over 10lb from the mouth of a tiny Devon river. He now begins this chapter.

AV Fresh water seems to attract bass. This is a fact which is now entrenched in bass-fishing lore. From a small stream trickling across the gritty sand of the beach to the expanse of a large estuary or drowned river valley, water of low salt content can be guaranteed to provide a focus for bass and bass anglers. For present purposes, sewers, unsavoury as they are, can be regarded as 'fresh' water.

Estuaries may be so small that there is barely a stream of water entering the sea at low tide (it may even flow completely under the beach). Large estuaries, like the Fowey in Cornwall, may provide permanent deep-water anchorages for big boats. With this amount of variation it is difficult to make too many generalisations about the subject.

It is a case of getting to know your estuary. If the river is a small one, you will be forced to take advantage of the tide and to fish when water is flooding into the inlet. In contrast, a larger body of brackish water may contain bass at any state of the tide, particularly in the lower reaches near the mouth. However, it is a common feature of most estuaries that as the 'salt wedge' of sea water is forced up under the fresh by the rising tide, so the bass advance further from the sea.

At low water bass are likely to be caught, by spinning or legering, at the entrance to a sizeable estuary. As the flood begins, the fish swim up river and you must follow them. Travelling on foot may be difficult because of extensive areas of soft mud or deep drainage channels inside the river mouth. It will often be a case for painstakingly working out the path followed by the fish by trial and error. By establishing at what stage of the tide the fish are to be found at a particular place, it will be possible to ambush them by fishing the correct period at each productive spot.

Rocky areas, sandbanks, gullies and places where the river channel approaches close to the upper shore can all hold bass for a time as they travel upstream searching for food. Not many types of animal are able to survive the drastic change from salt water to fresh water conditions in an estuary, but those which can are usually present in abundance. It is the vast numbers of shore crabs, prawns, ragworms, small eels, flounders and perhaps even trout and salmon smolts that the bass seek in these conditions.

Although they are essentially marine fish, bass will occasionally, move right up into fresh water, as catches – including some large fish – taken by anglers coarse fishing in tidal stretches of rivers testify. I know of several large bass, one of which was well into double figures, which were caught well into the River Taw, past Barnstaple, in Devon.

After high water, such bass leave the estuaries, travelling back along the same paths by which they entered. Again the angler may be able to intercept them at selected spots.

Currents in estuaries are often very strong, especially near the sea, and, when legering, a grip lead may be necessary. Spinning can also be productive from suitable vantage points, as can float fishing, if it proves possible. The latter method is particularly useful when bass are located in the shallow estuary creeks of some rivers, where currents are slower.

The most effective natural baits in brackish water are probably crab and ragworm. The former is effective for bottom fishing because the millions of shore crabs in every estuary take longer to devour their own kind, but make short work of worm or fish. Ragworm is a good float-fishing bait. Both crab and worm will also frequently be taken by flounders or eels, which abound in estuaries. Estuaries are important bass nurseries and many of the bass taken on leger tackle by anglers will be small. To avoid these schoolies, which often average about four years in age and half a pound in weight, and sort out the better fish, baits such as tiny flounders, lampreys or small eels should be used.

When you get to know your estuary it may sometimes be possible to choose an entirely local bait, selected because, first, it is known to be common in the area; second, other anglers have found it to be effective; and, third, experimental sessions have proved its value. For example, a number of large bass have been taken from the mouth of the River Lyn in North Devon by anglers spinning with small trout across the river mouth.

Great care is often required when fishing estuary marks. Strong currents, especially on the ebb, mean that there is a danger of being swept away if you fall in or attempt to wade a channel that is too deep. As the tide floods there is the additional risk of being cut off on banks isolated when water fills in channels or depressions behind you. The mud itself can be quite treacherous and it is foolish to explore recklessly on your own in a new area. When fishing a muddy shore, never stand still for too long in case your booted feet become embedded in the mud.

ML One of the first bass I ever caught was taken from the estuary of the little Silverburn, a stream running into the upper part of Castletown harbour in the Isle of Man. I was accustomed to catching trout and sea trout from the stream itself and one of the best tactics was light spinning. The lure was cast upstream and retrieved swiftly with the flow. Before it enters the harbour, the stream is held back by a concrete dam; as a result, the sea tops the dam only on big spring tides and, for long periods, the water upstream of the barrier is quite fresh.

Having observed fish 'rising' in the freshwater lagoon, I decided to extend my spinning operations downstream to investigate the cause. The result was not the expected trout, but several very small (8–10 inch) bass. No doubt similar situations can be found in other estuaries and in brackish lagoons associated with power stations and the like. Presumably tactics other than spinning would also take fish in these 'fresh' waters and, in fact, a keen coarse angler, Arthur Blatch, recounted the capture in years past of school bass on ragworm baits at Wareham on the Dorset

Frome. Wareham is just about the upper limit of saltwater incursion in the River Frome.

The estuary of the Hampshire Avon, famous for its coarse fish, salmon and trout, provides another interesting case. In some privately administered pools on the lower river silver bream, roach and bass can be seen in early summer, side by side between the mats of algae. Until a ban was imposed on the method, a few anglers caught numbers of very big bass by livebaiting with dace. The dace were presented, on freeline tackle, to fish which were visible in the clear chalk waters.

I believe (although I have no personal experience of it) that in summer, on big spring tides, the fry of freshwater fish are sometimes killed by incursions of freshwater to the lower reaches of rivers. Bass soon become aware of these opportunities and may be taken on small fish baits or lures from such places.

To return to the first point made in this chapter, why should streams of fresh water provide, if indeed they do, gathering points for bass? First, bass, like eels, mullet, trout and flounders, are able to tolerate the great stress imposed on them when they shift back and forth between fresh and salt water. This ability gives the fish access to the profusion of food mentioned earlier, but perhaps something more than this is involved. Even tiny trickles of water are reputed to attract the fish and these are unlikely to generate a well stocked larder of bass food. At risk of being called a heretic, could it possibly be that, in some cases, the little streams simply form a focus for bass anglers rather than for the fish themselves? There are certainly plenty of bass to be caught along open shores where there is not the slightest hint of freshwater inflow.

9
Pier Fishing

AV Whilst many anglers seem to regard pier fishing as synonymous with beginner's fishing, there is no way to ignore the fact that every year a lot of bass are caught from piers. Up and down the country local anglers, with expert knowledge of their piers, make regular catches of bass in season.

The reasons are not hard to find. Bass are chiefly inshore, shallow-water fish and piers are structures enabling baits to be easily placed where the fish are sheltering from the main current and feeding. A pier can, of course, be used simply as a fishing platform for casting to a known or suspected holding area of the surrounding seabed, for example a rock or weed patch; however, this chapter is about the piers themselves as holding areas.

The piers which have the best fishing are usually those that do not dry out at low water. If there is always some water under a pierhead, then there will be more seaweed growing on the piles, and plenty of shelter for small fish and crabs, prawns and other crustaceans. Bass will, according to the time of year, weather and appetite, frequent such areas, and then the angler, by using appropriate methods, can catch these fish. At times, very big bass are caught from piers; sometimes they have been deliberately angled for.

Piers that dry out at low water and solid stone piers are popular fishing venues and some of them produce fish consistently. However, the solid, jetty-type pier is best considered as a rocky headland, whilst the other type, visible as a bare skeleton at low tide, will vary in its fishing characteristics; often more will depend on the nature of the surrounding seabed than anything else.

Anyone who has spent a few hours investigating the life which is visible under a pier will realise the variety that can exist, even where the bottom is only sand. The piles serve as foundations for the different seaweeds, mussels, barnacles, limpets and hydroids, and, in their shelter, clinging to the woodwork or living in cracks, are a host of crustaceans, such as prawns, sea slaters and different types of crabs. Here too are many different small fish, secure in the more sheltered environment and feeding on the smaller animals present. The commonest fish are usually blennies, gobies, small pouting, poor cod, pollack, wrasse, pipefish, fifteen-spined stickle-backs, baby flatfish and, perhaps sandeels.

At low water the scour pools at the bases of the piles provide a refuge for prawns and small fish. All these organisms are food for larger fish such as conger, pollack and bass, and, if a pier is within the geographical range of bass, at some time or another they will

Positions taken up by bass and small bait fish in relation to the currents flowing round the structures of a pier.

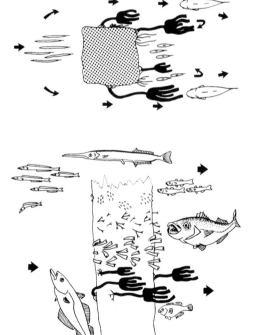

be there and their numbers may be large. I once saw many thousands of average-to-large bass in a shoal. I don't mean that I saw tails coming out of the sea or a lot of splashing, nor do I mean that I was swimming beneath the surface; from a pier, I actually saw thousands of bass together.

My father, myself and an angling acquaintance of the time had been fishing on Ryde pier during a night in July and, for some reason, we had stayed later than normal to fish the ebb, and we fished it in an unusual place. It was a warm summer night, with calm water, and I think it was one of those rare nights when we had caught nothing. We had used worms, prawns and sole-skin lures, but all to no avail. Why we had remained until dawn I cannot remember, but, as the light increased, we were fishing about thirty yards apart from the side of the pier that the current was leaving. This was the scene of the most amazing sight I have seen in the context of bass fishing.

The tide was ebbing and fast receding from Ryde sands; it was calm and the few feet of water remaining beneath us was crystal clear. As the light increased we could see that fish were swimming out with the tide, going through the pier from west to east, and they were visible as far to the left and right as we could see. There were so many that an estimate of numbers of fish is impossible, but for the best part of an hour there was an endless succession of bass in a tight shoal. We were all familiar with mullet and my father's friend was a mullet specialist, so there is no question of mistaken identity. These were bass, fish from medium size to well into double figures, and there were many thousands of them. They were not feeding, not breaking the surface, just swimming in a leisurely manner with the tide in the shallow water.

We tried everything we could to catch them, but we had no success. They were just not interested at all. If the water had been cloudy or it had been dark we would have had no indication of the vast numbers of fish there. The only contact that was made was by my father, using a piece of sole skin. One fish was briefly hooked, but it came off.

The experience was both frustrating and fascinating and, of course, I will never forget it. Looking back, I find several things of interest. First, there were no small fish; these were all mature bass. Second, they were in a large, dense shoal in the middle of the summer; they were not in small groups that might have been feeding in different places. Third, they were going somewhere; they were not interested at all in feeding. Perhaps they were keeping together in order to feed on some equally large shoal of small food-fish, but we saw no hint of feeding behaviour as they swam out and over the sand in three or four feet of water.

Bass are likely to be present around piers roughly from May till October and angling methods need to be varied to make the most of each part of the season. The bass will be found at various depths; usually the smaller fish are higher in the water than the larger ones, but sometimes very big bass are caught on baits fished at or near the surface.

Any of the methods known to be effective for bass can be used, but it is well to remember that the line needs to be able to withstand the chafing action of the piles and of the barnacles which encrust them. It may also have to cope with lifting a fish to safety if steps or a drop net are not available (but this should be only a last resort). Any angler intending to specialise in bass fishing from piers is advised to acquire a drop net. However, this does not mean that the rod needs to be an 8-foot broomstick. A 9-foot spinning rod is quite suitable, although a slightly shorter rod can be handy for fishing actually underneath a pier, on lower platforms where headroom is restricted. Steps, lower decks or launching ramps often permit the normal use of a net or gaff and, before commencing to fish, the first consideration should be whether access to such structures is possible.

Early in the season, during May and June, pier-haunting bass take worm baits well, particularly large king rag and white rag. More fish are taken if baits are fished above the bottom to avoid other, smaller, fish and the host of crabs waiting there to steal them.

The method which is most productive is drifting or simply dangling a large ragworm underneath the pier, searching the different levels until fish are found. A spinning rod is ideal for this because very little weight is required; simply fix a small weight about three feet from a 2/0 hook. Bass are usually found at the side of the pier which the current strikes and will generally be just beneath the pier waiting behind or slightly to one side of the piles.

In daylight the fish keep to the shade, unless chasing small fish such as sandeels, and they are usually a lot easier to tempt at night. A useful routine is to swing the tackle out into the current, let it sink down and under the pier and then, with the small weight only, the bait rises up and lies several yards behind your position and under the decking. The bait should then be slowly retrieved. Takes are usually positive, but quite often a fish can be felt to almost suck at the bait. When this happens, a very gentle lift will sometimes encourage the bass to take more positively, but equally often the fish will only remove the tail of the worm. This tail should then be replaced with another worm. Bass taken in mid-water (where most of them are) are seldom caught on a worm without an attractive moving tail. Takes are most frequent as the bait rises up from the bottom, or on the retrieve, and a sharp strike usually hooks the fish.

A variation on the same method involves the use of a live prawn. In high summer, when the bass are splashing about and not taking worms, prawn baits will often produce fish.

If peeler or soft crabs are available, they can be used in the same way as the other baits. Bass do not seem to find it odd to discover a crab suspended in mid-water, and it is a killing bait. However, it probably pays to fish crab on the bottom, as a bait to tempt a larger fish, since most mid-water bass in these situations are fish of less than 5lb.

Float fishing is also effective in these situations. A float will carry the bait to surface or mid-water feeding fish right under the middle of a pier. This method is fraught with dangers, however, since tackle losses can be frequent. The use of expendable floats such as old wine bottle corks is a good idea.

In such circumstances the float cannot be watched, of course, and the line is let out in small bursts, being held back every few seconds to make the bait rise up in the water in an attempt to induce a take. Bites are felt and must be struck immediately; then some luck is required.

Another evening in June twenty-odd years ago also sticks in my mind. At that time, as a teenager and keen angler I was keen to do my own thing and do it on my own, but not confident enough to be a solitary angler. So I fished with my father and, at the same time, always wanted to outdo him in the catching of fish.

This particular night, Dad and I cycled down the pier at Ryde on the Isle of Wight, and I think we were decidedly damp even before we saw the pier. It rained so hard that night and it never seemed to let up. We were well wrapped up, complete with sou'westers and oilskins, and the ragworm we had for bait were inside waterproof bags. The small amount of tackle required was carried in our pockets and, once on the pierhead, the usual routine was to tackle up and try various places where the fish might be, until the time was right for fishing 'down the railway'. (A train station with several tracks is still present on the east pier.)

At that time there was a dance-hall on the pierhead, and it was possible to fish from a veranda round this building; we used to float-fish into a triangle of open water in the middle of the pier. As the rain pelted down, we walked past the anglers who always fished on the bottom, catching mainly pouting with an occasional dogfish, and made for the veranda.

The dance-hall was full, but we were able to put the music far from our thoughts as we floated our baits across the triangle, right up to the piles at the other side, where we knew bass would be lying. I think the third member of the group that night, my father's friend Tom, arrived about then and the three of us fished, soaked, holding our light greenheart rods and centre-pin reels, feeling for the bites which we hoped would come.

In fact the night was good to us. We caught several bass from the veranda and one of them was a good one (which to us, as pier anglers, was then a fish of 3lb or more) – a fish of just on 4lb, which my father took. The soup was poured from the flasks at slack water, and we debated whether to call it a night and return home, still partly dry, with the half-dozen or so bass already taken, or to stay on and try for some more when the tide had turned towards the west. I think my youthful optimism may have had something to do with it, since, for whatever reason, we decided to stay.

During the soup, the tide turned and I discovered that my tackle had floated under the pier before I was aware of the change. In fact, I was made only too aware of my absence of mind when my ratchet screeched out and I struck into a fish, only to hear it splashing under the dance-hall. After some anxious moments, I had the bass beneath me and I handlined it up to the veranda. It was a twin to the fish my father had caught earlier.

With the tide turned, we made our way to the east side of the pier to fish into the current from there. With the late boat and the last train both departed, we made our way down by the railway track on the lower part of the pier, to fish beneath it. We were trespassing on British Rail property, but my father knew most of the porters and they were usually happy to let us fish there, provided we gave them a fish now and then. (The trains then were steam-powered; now the line is electrified and it is impossible to fish from the track.)

As the rain continued to pelt down, with the odd trickle making its way down the neck, into the cuff, or down wellington boots, we wondered just how mad we were. The rain was falling so heavily that it was difficult to see the lights of the street lamps on Ryde promenade, and only the conviction that fish would be caught encouraged us. I can remember how black and how wet the night was. I also remember how seldom it was that we failed to catch bass 'down the railway'; if we had landed bass beforehand, it was for sure we would get some more there.

We did catch more bass, and by the end of the session, with the tide ebbing, I know we tipped out our fish from the bags we used on to the station platform, to look at the catch. I did not keep a written record of catches then, but I know my three biggest bass totalled just under 12lb, and I had about eight fish. There was great satisfaction for me since I had caught more fish than Dad or Tom and, being young, I think I was able to ignore the weather more than they could. During these trips, it was virtually unknown to have a total blank and we caught bass regularly, as well as small pollack. The bass were usually between 1½lb and 4lb and the pollack averaged about 12oz.

I would never now keep fish as small as most of those we caught then, but at the time there seemed to be plenty of fish around, and if we caught bass of less than about a pound we always returned them, as we did most of the pollack.

In later years bass became more difficult to find from Ryde pier, and I fished all the other piers on the Isle of Wight, broadening my experience. Interestingly, the biggest two bass I was involved with from piers were both hooked when something different was being tried. On the first occasion I and a school friend, Roy, were fishing from the same veranda at low water – a time we never bothered with at that place usually. Roy hooked and played out a very good bass on a newly bought spinning rod and borrowed reel. The reel, however, only had 9lb line on it and, with the fish played out on the surface, we were faced with the problem of landing it. Sadly, with no one else around, we eventually tried to lift it. At first I seemed to pull about eight feet of line up and thought we would be all right. However, on looking over the edge, I saw that the fish was only just out of the water; obviously the line was stretching. Then it broke, and that was that. A fish of nine or ten pounds slowly swam away with hook and ragworm.

The other big fish was about the same size and I hooked it on a large piece of cuttlefish flesh from Totland pier, with the bait on the bottom. This time the fish was lost when an inexperienced friend tried to gaff it after firmly holding the trace in his hand. Of course the trace broke, and away went my best ever fish at the time. I nearly wept.

These two instances show several important things. First, always be sure you have the means to land a fish before you attempt to hook one. Second, even when you have a method which works well, always be prepared to experiment at different times of the tide and with different baits. Third, if someone else is with you, make sure they know how to assist if the occasion demands it.

Even though I don't often fish from piers these days, I still spend time peering under them; if I look carefully, I usually manage to find some good fish visible by the piles. Last summer I saw a very large bass underneath Ryde pier station as I waited with my wife and two small sons for a train.

In the middle months of July and August bass are sometimes difficult to tempt. They are more likely to take crab than worm, and occasionally will appear preoccupied, at the surface, with feeding on small fish. When prawn and crab fail to produce fish, spinning is worth a try, but if light lines are used tackle losses are almost bound to be heavy, since bass, although not usually fish to seek snags, are quite likely to swim between pier supports and the line then contacts the piles. A very attractive (and cheaper) bait than expensive spoons or spinners is a strip of fish, such as mackerel or garfish. This can be hooked through one end if it is less than three inches long, but should be arranged with the hook in the middle if it is longer.

If it is possible to obtain live sandeels, these are excellent summer pier-fishing baits – freelined, or drifted using a light lead, or float-fished. The sandeel can be lip hooked or hooked in the belly via the mouth and gill-cover.

A method which I have not tried in recent years, but one which my father used to great effect, taking many fish up to 9½lb, is 'spinning' a sole-skin lure on the surface at night. The piece of sole skin, roughly fish-shaped, is hooked at one end and moved through the water either by casting out and retrieving steadily or by working the lure directly underneath the rod tip in a figure-of-eight pattern. When the latter method is used, the best place to choose is near a pier light. (We often used to improvise a light by tying a torch to the railings to shine on the water.) Bass in the vicinity gradually seem to become aware of the lure – possibly repeated movement gives an impression of many active bait fish – and eventually the bass start slashing at it. I remember many evenings when the only fish caught were bass taken on a sole-skin lure fished in this manner. Anyone interested in trying this method for the first time should not be put off by the appearance of dry sole skin; when it is wetted it becomes extremely pliable, but remains very tough. The white belly skin is obtained from a fishmonger (or by catching your own sole), dried and then cut into strips. Feathers, muppets and streamer flies should work in the same way.

During the days when I did a lot of fishing from various piers on the Isle of Wight, although our group caught a great many bass, the really big fish were usually taken by anglers bottom-fishing with big baits of fish, squid or cuttlefish. At the time I was young and had neither the patience nor confidence to give up the tactics which I knew regularly produced fish for a less active method. Bottom fishing was unable to satisfy our hunting instinct, for we spent a lot of time trying this place and that during different states of the tide to find fish in mid-water. This to me *was* bass fishing.

We prided ourselves on knowing where fish would be at a particular state of the tide, but occasionally we would feel envious of a large bass taken by someone else on a bottom-fished bait.

If I were to spend a lot of time pier fishing these days, I would certainly put in plenty of hours using large baits fished on the bottom. For the pier angler with the larger fish on his mind, the best tactic must be bottom fishing right under the pier or next to the piles with a large crab or fish bait – and I do mean *large*. As a rough guide, a bait with a bulk less than that of a matchbox is too small. A big bass can take the largest soft shore crab with ease; a five-inch fish, a six-inch strip of cuttlefish, or a whole calamari-sized squid are equally acceptable alternatives.

The problem with this type of fishing is primarily that the bait may be taken by other fish, particularly conger (less chance of that if crab is used), but should there be a big bass in the vicinity it's odds on that the large bait will interest it; a worm bait probably will not. Then be ready for action, and have your net handy!

The most likely tactic to succeed with really large bass in such situations is a paternostered livebait. Sandeel, sand-smelt, pouting, wrasse and almost any other small fish are extremely attractive to these really big fish. A very ingenious method which has produced many good bass was developed in the south-east of England. This is the use of floating dead pouting, particularly at night. The fish are injected with air from a hypodermic syringe and then freelined on the surface. Some very large fish have been taken by this method, which is most often used from piers.

Every pier is, of course, different, but some additional hints may prove useful. In general the best times are when the tide flows strongly, and particularly during the first of the increasing flow in a new direction following slack water, although fish may be caught at any state of the tide. (Slack water, with no real flow, may not coincide with low and high waters; often the direction of the current changes during the ebb or flood, depending on geographical location. In any case the new flow seems to be a good time.) Gradually, as you come to understand your pier intimately, there is great satisfaction in knowing where fish are likely to be during the different stages of the tide.

Bass are usually easiest to catch at the beginning and end of the season, during May and June, and then again in September and October. It is almost always best for fishing natural baits if the water is not too clear, and often it is better if the sea is choppy; in general a very rough sea is not much good, and may even be dangerous on some piers.

It is frequently difficult to gather bait from a pier, but little pouting (at night) and wrasse (in daytime) can often be caught next to the piles by using small paternostered baits. Also, especially at low water, prawns can be gathered, from May onwards, by netting around the bases of the piles. At night the eyes of prawns glow brilliantly red if a torch is shone into the water. This can make prawning at night a practicable proposition, since a quick flash with a light will pick out the location of every prawn in the vicinity.

Frequently, even when mid-water fishing, fish other than bass may be taken. Those most commonly caught are small pollack, scad, garfish and mackerel, in about that order (with some variation from pier to pier). At times, large numbers of these may be taken, whereas the number of bass caught will rarely exceed about a dozen fish. (My own best effort was fifteen fish, with an average size of about 2lb.) Usually two or three bass are reason enough to feel pleased. On many occasions I have been unable to resist giving attention to other fish that were obviously present. When using a light rod there is plenty of enjoyment in taking mackerel, garfish or scad, which are usually easier to catch than bass anyway. For example, having initially intended to fish for bass, I recall on one occasion taking 63 pollack; 36 scad was the catch on another trip and 22 garfish on another. Even now, when I concentrate wholeheartedly on bass fishing in the summer, I could be tempted to try for other fish if I failed in my main intention.

American scientists have studied the effect of submerged mid-water artificial structures (for example pier piles) on the deployment of forage fish and predators. The predators were not bass but king mackerel and little tunny; however, the principles are exactly the same. Many small bait-fish took advantage of the 'bow-wave effect' upstream of the piles, holding station in the quiet water, whilst smaller numbers of little fish sheltered behind the structures. The predators took up their stations further downstream of the piles or closer to the seabed, positions from which they could strike at any fish which became separated from the protection of the schools. Multiple structures, such as piers, were found to attract and concentrate fish much more effectively than single structures, such as isolated rocks, and differences were observed in the species of fish found at different depths. Apparently fish very rapidly moved in to congregate round newly introduced structures. These conclusions confirm the notion of pier piles or bridge supports forming a focus for different fish, and the predators seem to take up station in exactly the same way as bass around pier piles.

Using artificial lures from piers or bridges is essentially similar to lure fishing in other situations. It usually pays to fish close to the supporting structures, bearing in mind that the bass will usually be in positions sheltered from the main flow. By using small pirks, German sprats or 'willow-leaf' spoons according to the strength of flow (the heavier lures will generally be needed when the tide is flowing swiftly), it is possible to fish more or less vertically downwards or to let the current carry the lure between the piles. The best type of lure action is the one which produces the most realistic swimming action on the drop. The basic principles of spinning – which involve needle-sharp hooks, a very firm strike and careful representation of the size, shape, colour and movement of the acceptable prey – all apply.

The use of strings of feathers, muppets or even Redgills, jigged above a lead (or a pirk), is favoured in some areas. Dave Bourne of Dover, a skilled exponent of lure fishing, says that one method used from his local breakwater involves two or three Redgills fished up the line, using a sink-and-draw method along the sides of the wall. Bass caught on lures from this mark tend to come after dark. This last point seems significant, and sole-skin lures fished in this way could certainly pay off handsomely. Dave says of the effectiveness of night-time spinning: 'I think that this is mostly because the bass feed on the surface after dark, which makes it easier to spin for them, rather than trying to work a lure near the bottom during daylight when you are about fifty feet above where the bass are feeding, on the bottom in a 3- or 4-knot tide.'

It seems likely that, in strong flows of water such as that described above, a paternostered plug or livebait could be very effective. By altering the lengths of the links on the paternoster it would be possible to fish at various distances from the seabed.

Fishing from bridges which have supporting pillars in deep, strong tidal flows is not very different from angling from many piers. Prawn fished on light float or paternoster gear is the local bait in Dorset (where Mike fishes) and many of the bass taken in this way are small. The structures shelter huge shoals of sand-smelts, wrasse and other small fish, and bass can be caught on pirks, spoons and plugs, as well as on small live fish. In fact, some of the livebaits which have been used with success are rather unusual, being small (6–8 inches) freshwater eels and lampreys obtained from the local river. Eels tend to wriggle and twist up the traces, but brook lampreys and their eel-like larvae are long-lived and well behaved baits.

Mike says that in many hours spent fishing from these bridges, it was unusual to catch a bass weighing more than a few pounds, using any method. A bass in the middle teens of pounds did follow an Abu Killer plug almost to the rod tip on one occasion, but it rejected the imitation with all the disdain it could muster.

This chapter closes with some information contributed by Dave Bourne of the Dover Sea Angling Association. Every year this club spends a week bass fishing from the Southern Breakwater and the accompanying record of catches shows just what can be achieved by experienced locals.

Table 3 Bass Caught from the Southern Breakwater by DSAA Members

Year	[No. of Bass]	[Aggregate Weight (lb)]	[Notable fish (lb oz)]
1955	131	200	?
1956	222	346	5.8
1957	102	266	5.15¾, 5.8½, 5.8
1958	75	254	8.1½, 8.1
1959	45	155	6.7½
1960	32	126	8.6½, 7.6¾
1961	54	149	6.3½, 5.13
1962	57	151	7.8, 7.4, 7.2¾
1963	28	90	7.8, 6.4
1964	41	105	6.5, 6.4
1965	38	124	7.5, 6.14
1966	46	144	10.14, 7.6
1967	27	97	9.12½, 7.7½
1968	21	94	10.15
1969	23	86	8.1, 7.14½
1970	17	84	11.8, 10.2, 9.5, 9.0, 8.12, 8.6
1971	14	60	8.4, 8.3
1972	44	171	10.15
1973	27	129	12.7½
1974	17	70	8.5, 7.1
1975	20	95	10.8, 9.9, 9.4½
1976	45	240	12.8¾, 11.9½, 10.0, 9.15, 9.7½, 9.5, 9.14, 8.15
1977	14	55	8.15½, 7.4, 6.11
1978	31	110	10.13, 8.8
1979	?	?	?
1980	22	77	7.7½
1981	33	81	—
1982	25	82	10.1½, 10.1¼
1983	43	134	8.7½, 7.3
1984	56	203	8.6½
1985	53	160	—
1986	38	122	—
1987	47	153	12.12, 8.10, 8.4, 8.2

10
Where and When to Fish

To put it at its shortest, the bass season begins at about the middle of April, and ends in October . . . Generally speaking the best months of all are May, June, September and October.

Clive Gammon, *Sea Fishing*, 1969

ML When I first came to live in the south of England I had seen very few bass, and caught even fewer. Like any keen angler, I sniffed out all the local tackle shops to glean what scraps of information I could. During one such visit I had the good fortune to meet 'Mr Wheeler', as I then knew him. He was the manager of the fishing tackle section in Beales, a large Bournemouth department store. Clarence Wheeler's knowledge of bass angling was profound; he claimed to have been the first importer of Rapala plugs in Britain. Initially the plugs were imported for his own use and he employed them, along with other methods, to catch a great many large bass from the race at the mouth of Poole Harbour and from the lifting bridge of the harbour itself.

In the many hours which I spent, leaning on the counter of the shop, discussing fishing in general, and bass in particular, one comment stuck in my mind. 'The second spring tides in May are the time to start bass fishing!' he used to say. Now, as in any other form of fishing, the time of the year, the state of the tidal cycle and the time of day when fish can or cannot be caught varies a good deal. It varies from area to area and from year to year, but how can you decide whether it is worth going bass fishing or not? Is it possible that there are any rules which will work wherever you happen to be fishing?

What sort of things control the movements and feeding activities of the bass? The most obvious factor which affects the seasonal activities of living things is the length of the day. Every year, with great precision, the days lengthen regularly until 21 June, when the period of daylight is longest. After midsummer they again shorten until 21 December. Both plants and animals use this regular cycle as a timer because it is much more reliable than things like the amount of sunshine or the temperature. Even cool, dull, summer days are just as long as their counterparts in a blazing hot year, and the days of a warm, bright winter spell – if it ever occurred – would be just as short as usual.

Because the length of the day is such a dependable calendar, it is often the signal which tells plants and animals when they should be resting, feeding or breeding. For example, in autumn, chrysanthemum growers use artificial light to fool their plants into 'thinking' that the days are still long. This delays flowering and gets the flowers in the shops for Christmas. Egg producers use a similar trick to keep the hens laying.

It is likely that the basic yearly cycle of the bass is regulated by changes in day length. After the mature fish have spawned, the crop of eggs and sperm for the following year begin to develop. The hormones of the fish, in response to these seasonal changes, ensure that development is completed by the following year or thereabouts. The basic growth and behaviour pattern is then modified by the influence of temperature. The warmer it is, the quicker events proceed – within limits. Following a mild winter and a warm spring, the bass may spawn a week or two earlier than usual and, if the sea is cold, things may be delayed into June. Because the sea may be a couple of degrees warmer in the English Channel than on the Welsh coast or in the Thames estuary, it is probable that, in some years at least, bass in Cornwall and Devon spawn earlier than those further north or east.

To the bass angler, the time when fish gather just prior to spawning may be the first great opportunity of the year. Don Kelley – that mine of information about bass – writing in 1949 summed things up more or less as follows: 'Late in April large shoals of mature fish begin to appear at certain favoured marks . . . The bass remain in these large shoals for a few weeks, then split up into smaller groups of half a dozen or so and roam the adjoining coasts in search of food.' So here we have one valuable indication of a chance to capitalise on concentrations of large, mature fish. My own observations confirm Don's remarks.

In the same article, Don makes a second important point about seasonal movements with which I am again in total agreement. To quote: 'In October they re-form into large shoals at their spring rendezvous and shortly afterwards move offshore and disappear until the following April.'

To fill in this picture of the yearly movements of mature bass there are studies which were carried out on the south and west coasts of Great Britain and in the coastal waters of the Irish Republic. Like many other species of fish, bass are known to migrate from place to place as the seasons change. Early studies suggested that it was rather a stay-at-home species, with local populations restricted to short stretches of coastline. It may be, in fact, that the fish have a homing instinct and tend to return to their 'own' region, be it Anglesey or Cornwall, Dorset or Essex. Support is lent to this viewpoint by some observations made by Alan. He noticed that bass from North Wales virtually always had little brown parasitic worms in the meat. These nematodes are easily visible when the fish is steaked or filleted for cooking and, in our experience, are much less common in bass from other areas, suggesting that the population belongs to that one area only.

It now seems certain that there is a general movement of bass in the autumn towards the south and west, to the offshore waters of the British Isles. This migration is probably triggered off by the combination of shortening days and falling water temperatures.

The actual time when bass leave an area in the autumn may vary from place to place. Whereas the fish of North Wales or Essex may go as early as mid-October, those of Dorset, Devon and Cornwall probably hang on well into November or even December in mild winters. Similarly the fish may return in April to the south-west coast, but as late as June to areas further north or east.

With the exception of small, immature fish, which may remain in estuaries throughout the year, the above pattern more or less sets out the season for worthwhile bass angling.

The occasional large – even very large – fish caught in winter (December–March) every year may be, as Don Kelley has suggested, 'a few solitary fish – unfit specimens or members of weak year classes [which] appeared to remain throughout the winter'.

Is it possible to narrow down the limits of the bass angling season any further than 'some time from April to November'? Of course it is. But to do so each of us must make tricky decisions which depend on an intimate knowledge of our own patch. One thing is certain – it is rarely, if ever, absolutely hopeless for bass fishing. The secret of regular success is, first, to explore your local shoreline for the sort of conditions described in this book; second, to fish each spot with a range of appropriate methods throughout the year; and, third, to try to fish every place at as many phases and states of the tide and weather conditions as possible. By keeping a note of successes and failures related to time, tide, weather, place and method you will vastly increase your chances of success.

Exposed Ledge at low water.

11
Some Successful Venues

Hard-earned knowledge about where and when bass can be caught is not to be given away lightly. However, we think that by describing some places where we have made good catches, important points can be made. Significant features of our venues are to be found on many other shores; perhaps they may help you find some good places. The marks described in this chapter are all real places; however, searching the Ordnance Survey maps for the names would be a fruitless exercise.

The diagrams are intended to supplement the descriptions and photographs. On each plan a star or stars give some idea of a suitable stance and the distance in yards at which fish may be expected is arrowed; shorter casts will often produce fish. Black arrows show the main run of the tidal currents and the way in which fish may be distributed is also indicated. The relationship to tidal conditions is shown by a broken line. HWST means high water spring tides and so on. If it is thought to be helpful a section along the direction of a cast straight out from the shore is included. For clarity each of us has initialled his respective venues.

QUIET BAY, ISLE OF WIGHT (AV)

Description

Rocky beach with some sandy patches, facing south-east, fairly shallow, with some boulders and stones covered by wrack.

Time and Tide

The mark fishes on spring tides from HW$-1\frac{1}{2}$ to HW$-\frac{1}{2}$ (the best hour) and then until HW$+1$.

I have fished this mark at night only, since it is visited by various

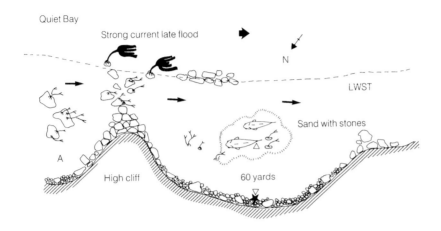

Quiet Bay

Strong current late flood

N

LWST

Sand with stones

A

High cliff

60 yards

Quiet Bay, Isle of Wight – a very productive bass mark.

people by day and I have wanted to avoid publicity. It has been a very reliable beach and I never found anyone else fishing it. I suspect that bass would also be caught in daytime.

Tackle and Method

I always use my standard running leger here, with a 3-foot trace and a short link to the lead. From HW − 1½ until HW, 3– 4oz of lead are needed if 18–20lb line is used. Tackle losses are occasional until HW, but then the current increases, 5 or 6oz of lead are needed, and tackle losses are heavy as the gear is pulled into snags.

Bait

Crab or fish baits are equally effective here. I have used all sorts of crabs and mainly wrasse as fish-baits, but have also taken a few fish on cuttle.

Weather and Conditions

This venue produces fish if it is calm or choppy but not if the water is gin-clear, nor if it is rough. Fresh to strong winds from the south to north-east render it unfishable.

165

Other Comments

I have taken many bass in the 3–8lb bracket, with two over 9lb. Bites are typical: there are as many slack-line bites as pulls away. With slack-line bites the fish may swim right to the water's edge before dropping the bait or getting hooked.

Very few other fish are taken. Occasionally a conger gets hooked, rarely a pouting or rockling.

The mark was remarkable since the fish arrived, if they were going to (and this mark was very reliable), within fifteen minutes of a certain rock 'going down'. The bass kept so well to this timetable that for several years I could time my arrival very efficiently and know from the first cast whether or not I would catch fish.

It is interesting since the 'basin' (which first attracted me) and the large rocks to the left create a region where the water moves

Sheltered Ledge, Isle of Wight – a typical shallow-water rock mark which fishes well to legered crab or fish baits.

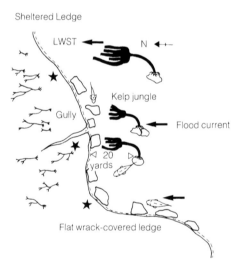

only slowly to the right when the main current is strong. The fish seem to come into the bay to keep out of the main run, and they feed well until HW; when the current then picks up the chances of getting fish diminish. Bites after HW tend to be the one-huge-pull type and I find these difficult to hit. On a typical spring tide there is about eight feet of water over the basin at HW.

Sadly the cliff has fallen down now and the shape of the seabed has altered so that the flow is different. The fish do not now seem to arrive regularly as the tide floods and I am still looking for a mark as good as this has been. It was one of my best places. However, I still catch a few bass from position A as soon as the large rocks become covered.

SHELTERED LEDGE, ISLE OF WIGHT (AV)

Description

An extensive rocky ledge facing east and quite sheltered. Weed cover is complete and there is kelp jungle all around the edge and further out.

Time and Tide

The ledge only uncovers on low water spring tides and can therefore only be fished then for an absolute maximum of one and a half hours down and two hours up, at night (or by day if the water is dirty).

Tackle and Method

The water is shallow and very weedy and the best method is legering. Heavy tackle is useless and a lead of 1oz running on 15lb line cast up to 25 yards with a spinning rod is a successful method.

Bait

Crab is good at night or during daytime in the early part of the season, but during late spring and summer wrasse are abundant and almost invariably the first to grab a crab bait in daylight. Fish baits are also good: wrasse are excellent and I have also taken bass on blenny, cuttlefish and squid.

Weather and Conditions

As long as the water is not clear, the bass can be caught. In rough weather the fish are probably not there and fishing is impossible. Weed quickly becomes suspended and makes fishing very difficult for several days after a blow, but as soon as it settles the fishing is good. On the other hand, an easterly wind is good when producing a slight chop. Many of my best days have been in flat calm conditions.

Other Comments

Access is difficult and dangerous, especially at night. Bass of all sizes are taken. Occasionally conger are hooked. The bass swim right in the edge and lack of cover means that a low profile and stealth are vital. Fish must be netted on to the ledge. It is important to keep an eye on a gully behind which fills and can cut off retreat. Most anglers would be very surprised at the delicacy of a typical bass take in this place, but, once the bites are familiar, bass can be taken with great regularity when conditions are suitable.

GRITTY BEACH, DORSET (ML)

Description

A beach facing south-east, made of fine grit and shingle in an angle of the cliff, sloping into shallow water and sheltered by an offshore wrack-covered reef. At low tide there is from two to three feet of water with a mixed bottom of grit, sand, mud and weed fragments, with the odd large stone or boulder and, twenty yards out, a thin bed of wrack growing on stones.

Time and Tide

The flooding tide runs gently from west to east and the beach fishes well on flooding neap tides and at LW. I have caught bass on

Gritty Beach, Dorset – at low water neap tides very big bass patrol the margin of the pebbly strand.

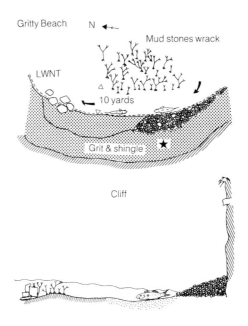

this beach throughout the summer months and at all times of day, with the dusk period being particularly productive.

Tackle, Baits and Methods

My pals and I have caught quite a few large bass very close in, by freelining with crab, squid, sandeel or ragworm close to the sea's edge. Spinning tackle, with lines of 8–12lb BS, is quite suitable for margin fishing. Hooks should be large, wide in the gape (4/0–6/0), well sharpened and leaving plenty of point and barb exposed, whatever bait is in use. The fish often pick up the bait quite softly and then move briskly away from the shore taking five, ten, fifteen or twenty yards of line, if they are offered no resistance. Before striking I allow the bass to draw the line tight and then hit them hard. Fish are quite often missed on the strike and, since they may be very large bass, this can be extremely frustrating.

On occasions, when the wind blows onshore and waves stir up the shallow seabed, colouring the water, small school bass will be present along this beach and can readily be caught on legered

169

baits. Crab or worm lobbed out to the edge of the wrack bed will tempt wrasse of all sizes.

Spinning with floating plugs will also catch big bass along this beach. The best tactic seems to be stalking quietly along the shore, scanning the sea ahead with polaroids to cut down the glare and casting beyond any fish spotted.

Piles of weed sometimes accumulate along the drift line on the shingle and, when these piles are present, bass and mullet will feed on maggots at high water of spring tides.

Weather and Conditions

In calm conditions (flat calm), very large bass are often visible in the margins of the sea, patrolling back and forth along fifty yards of beach, within a foot or two of the water's edge. Great care is needed to avoid scaring the fish.

BOULDER BEACH, DORSET (ML)

Description

A rocky, south-facing, gently sloping beach, thickly littered between low and high tide marks with big boulders. Below the low water mark the boulders are more scattered and thickets of wrack clothe the bedrock.

Time and Tide

This mark fishes best on spring tides from HW−1 to HW+1 but bass can be caught at any time when the water is more than a couple of feet deep. Fish are present along this beach, and others like it, throughout the season. I have records of many large bass up to 13 pounds in weight caught along this short stretch.

Tackle, Baits and Methods

Most anglers fishing from these boulders use simple, heavy leger or paternoster tackle. Fishing in this way produces patchy results. I have found light spinning gear, with line of 8 or 10lb BS, a small

Boulder Beach. A potential graveyard for tackle but easily fished with buoyant plugs.

Boulder Beach, Dorset – at first glance this might be considered unfishable but at high water spring tides it can be productive to either lures or bait.

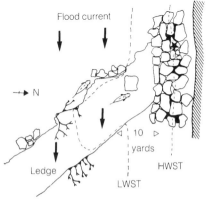

171

link swivel and a floating plug or plastic eel, to be very effective. The slightly heavier forms of plastic or wooden plugs allow longer casts and fish rather deeper than the standard Rapala floaters, giving some advantages. Deep-diving or sinking lures are not recommended, being easily snagged and lost in these conditions. I examine the area at low water to avoid loss of lures.

In daytime, crab and worm baits will attract countless wrasse; from dusk onwards mackerel, sandeel and other baits may tempt bass, rockling and the occasional conger. Artificials of the type mentioned are reliable attractors for bass of all sizes. Good wrasse and pollack also take lures over this mark and mullet may be present in large numbers at times. Bass and mullet often associate together.

Weather and Conditions

Clear or coloured water, calm or rough conditions all produce bass. Sometimes the water may be full of bits of weed, making

Flat Ledge, Dorset – with the right approach such ledges can be the best bass marks of all.

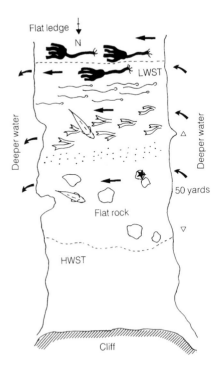

spinning difficult. Strong onshore winds build up a heavy surf and make any sort of fishing almost impossible.

FLAT LEDGE, DORSET (ML)

Description

A flat limestone ledge, sloping gently seawards, facing south and projecting well beyond the surrounding shoreline. It is more or less bare, but with zones of wrack, thong-weed and kelp at the extreme seaward end. The sides of the ledge are more or less sheer, falling into kelp-filled gullies, filled with water even at low tide.

Time and Tide

This ledge fishes best from May to June and from October to November, particularly from LW to HW; it is not usually much good on the ebb. Dawn is generally best with dusk a close second.

Tackle, Bait and Method

The way I dress for this type of venue is to wear appropriately warm clothing, waterproof jacket, waders and overtrousers (worn outside the waders) to keep me dry when surf overtops the waders. (Now we always wear chest waders – we must have been crackers!) This is an almost inevitable occurrence when trying to fish from a vantage point. When wading, I am very careful on wet, smooth, brown rock surfaces and greyish, slimy bottoms of pools – both are almost friction free and impossible to stand on. Using spinning gear with 8 or 10lb line, I cast a floating plug straight out to sea (20–30 yards should be possible and more than adequate) and retrieve just fast enough to make the lure vibrate the rod tip. Since the flow of the tide across the ledge is strong, a very slow retrieve (or none at all) is often suitable.

Hooks are kept *very* sharp and it is essential to check them after contact with rock, barnacles or wrasse. I check the line after any snag. In the event of a hang-up, I give slack line immediately and the plug usually floats free. If snagged on kelp or weed, a gentle steady pull (by hand) generally frees the lure, but watch out for it catapulting back into your face. With care, all but the largest fish can be beached on this tackle by sliding them ashore.

I often see fish turning or slashing on the surface over flat ledges. In ideal conditions, with plenty of fish about, a *small* Rapala or Redgill sometimes produces more bites. If I suspect that fish are further out, I clip on a heavier plug, such as a Nils Master Invincible or, in desperation, a small Toby, Krill or Tobis, which makes it necessary to wind like hell. At this stage tackle loss becomes almost inevitable.

Weather and Conditions

Large numbers of bass may be present on ledges of this type when there is a reasonable surf, provided the water is not filthy or full of drifting weed fragments. Warm onshore winds ranging from about force 3 to force 7 produce the right sort of conditions.

Other Comments

This ledge, and others like it, provide some of the best bass fishing I have ever experienced, particularly in early summer. Under calm conditions this venue generally produces wrasse or nothing. The

Worbarrow Bay, Dorset – a wide variety of productive bass territories.

wrasse will often take plugs well in late summer and autumn at half-flood upwards and they may snag the tackle. Pollack can sometimes be taken at dusk in summer. I have never used bait over the ledge, but float-fished sandeel, prawn or small live fish could be effective.

Alan says he feels confident that legering with big baits would also produce fish here.

PS

We have now fished this ledge and a similar one with crab and fish baits following Alan's instructions and in about ten man-hours of angling the results are bass of 8¼lb, 7½lb, 6½lb, and 1½lb, a wrasse of about 2lb and two missed bass bites.

WORBARROW TOUT, DORSET (ML)

Description

There are steep rock surfaces dropping into ten or twenty feet of water with heavy kelp growth along the rock edges and the shallower ledges.

Time and Tide

Bass may be present on this mark at any time or state of the tide, but since it lies within army firing ranges it is not often accessible.

Tackle, Baits and Methods

Good bass have been caught on bottom tackle baited with squid or fish. Spinning with plugs, spoons and plastic eels is also productive.

I well remember the first time I fished this spot. Terry Gledhill and I were walking back along the shore, making for our car, when a young man in a black leather motor-bike outfit came towards us. He was clearly in a hurry and in his right hand was a spinning rod rigged up with a slim Toby spoon. Despite his hurry, he stopped for a yarn about the fishing. It was clear that he was

*Worbarrow Tout, Dorset –
often closed to the public,
the steep rock faces and
deep water produce bass
when the sea is rough.
Generally these rocks are
dangerous to fish from in
such conditions.*

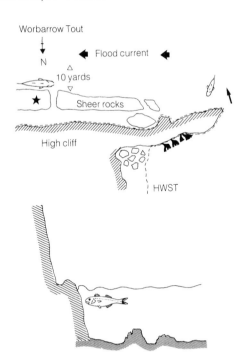

very knowledgeable and it transpired that, in previous years, he
had taken quite a few bass to 13½lb from the deep water by
spinning. He now lives many miles away, but returns to fish
whenever he has the chance.

Weather and Conditions

It has proved difficult to predict when this mark will fish well, but
very large bass can be caught in both rough and calm seas. In
rough weather the ledges are unfishable but one of our best bass
catches was taken when the sea was a mass of white foam; the bass
were in the six to seven pound class and took a spoon.

Other Comments

This headland reef drops off directly into deep water and, because
of this, provides a considerable range of species. Bass are by no
means the commonest fish. The other fish that can be caught here
(on appropriate baits and tackle) include pollack, conger, wrasse,
scad, mackerel and garfish.

SOUTH DEVON COVE, (ML)

Description

A small, cliff-backed cove between high rocky ledges and facing south. The beach consists solely of fine, clean sand out to and beyond normal casting range (with any sort of tackle). Apart from the rock walls on either side the only features are isolated patches of rock sticking up from the sand, and a small freshwater stream running into the middle of the bay.

Time and Tide

Bass swim into the cove at HW−3 and stay until the start of the ebb. If the water is reasonably clear the smaller fish may be visible in schools swimming over the sand; larger fish tend to hang about the rocky islands and prominences.

Sandy Cove, Devon – after dark and when the sea is rough big bass move in to feed.

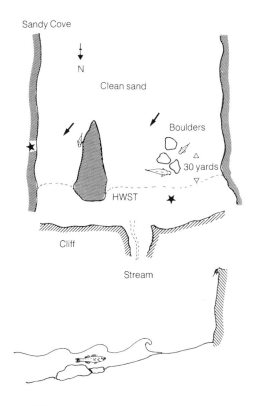

177

Tackle, Baits and Methods

Light leger tackle is appropriate for this beach and the bass will take live or frozen sandeel well.

Weather and Conditions

The best fishing conditions are when the sea is coloured after an onshore blow. A rolling sea and a thick suspension of sand in the water bring the bass into this bay to feed, particularly as the tide floods. When it is clear, the fish may be present but are only likely to take well after dark.

Other Comments

Although my experience is limited, this venue is striking for the lack of interest evoked by the use of spinners. Despite spinning with plugs, plastic eels and spoons when bass were clearly visible, I never even managed to induce a follower.

EXPOSED LEDGE, SOUTH-EAST WALES (AV)

Description

An exposed rocky shore, facing south, with boulders at high water and extensive bare ledges extending out past low water.

Time and Tide

The best time we have found is at half-ebb on spring tides when the water is forced up and over the bigger ledges and a strong current created.

Bait

Crab has produced the best results. There are a lot of small conger and rockling present, which are two reasons for not using fish baits.

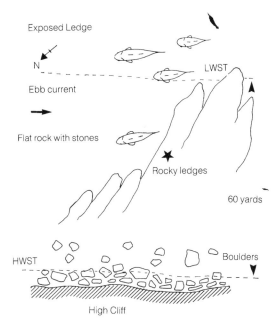

Exposed Ledge, South Wales – as in many other places, the bass are caught over only a short period when a strong ebb tide is flowing on to the ledges.

Tackle and Method

Light running leger tackle using leads of 1–2oz and suitable light rod.

Weather and Conditions

Bass are caught in calm or choppy seas.

Other Comments

The bass are present in numbers only when there is a strong flow over the bigger ledges. For whatever the reason the fish are found only for a short time. This is typical of most rocky bass marks: the fish are there at their own time, and you need to discover it by trial and error. Bass like strong currents and most good places have strong currents, but I suspect that here the bass are holding station in slack water down under the ledges, perhaps waiting for food to be washed over their heads or towards them.

179

THE HOLE, NORTH WALES (AV)

Description

A sheltered rocky shore with a deep channel close in. There is extensive cover by weed and a kelp jungle from the spring low water mark downwards. The ebb and flood currents are very strong.

Time and Tide

I have taken bass here on the late ebb, low water and flood tide up to half-flood. The best time is from low water for the first hour of the flood. Spring tides are better and make it easier to cast into the channel at low water.

The Hole, North Wales – another productive low-water mark which fishes best on spring tides.

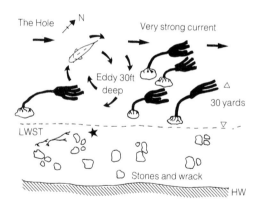

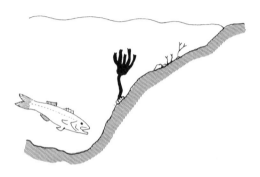

Tackle, Bait and Method

Spinning accounts for a few fish but the best method is legering. The bottom is foul with rocks and kelp and the strong current means that heavy line is needed. I use 28lb main line and 23lb trace and lead link. I use a 5-foot trace here. Leads up to 5 or 6oz are required. Lobs of up to forty yards are needed, with a light or medium beach rod.

The only worthwhile bait is crab; big edible crab baits are easily the best.

Weather and Conditions

Weather does not affect the fishing. There is no wave action to speak of.

Other Comments

The bass are of a very high average size and make it worthwhile using the heavy tackle. My biggest bass was taken here and I have had many other good ones.

This mark is included since it illustrates the point that bass will concentrate where an eddy makes it easier to hold station and also because most fish are taken – unusually – in relatively deep water. The eddy also makes bite detection easier. More fish are caught by using a long trace with this heavy tackle. Codling and conger are also present.

This is a most unusual mark, but typical of those found in the Menai Straits between Bangor and Port Dinorwic, where many very big bass have been taken.

ABER, NORTH WALES (AV)

Description

A north-facing sandy, muddy beach, very near the mouth of a river. The beach shelves extremely gently; there is a small pebble beach at high water.

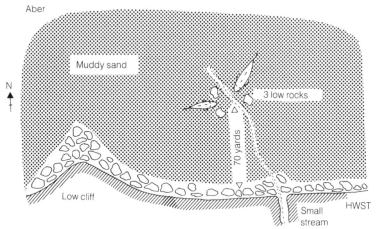

Aber, North Wales – a very reliable soft-bottom mark which fishes best in calm conditions.

Time and Tide

It is only worth fishing here on spring tides from HW−2 to HW+2 at night. The best time is the first hour of ebb.

Tackle, Bait and Method

Light leger tackle; there is no current to speak of, and the lack of snags means that any tackle that can be cast about seventy yards is sufficient. Use ragworm or crab (any) for bait.

Weather and Conditions

It must be calm – either no wind or a light offshore wind.

Other Comments

The stream may concentrate fish here, as may the low, flat rocks. When conditions are right this mark is very reliable and the bass are usually of medium size (2–5lb). The biggest bass I know of from here was 8½lb, but one night I hooked a real monster which broke my 10lb trace.

Flounders are also present and occasionally small eels are a nuisance.

12
Dreams Do Come True

To show what can happen when a bass angler gets everything right, each of us has described a special day. The differences between the two accounts are, perhaps surprisingly, more striking than the similarities. Days such as these do not occur once a week, once a month, or even once a year, but any serious bass angler should be prepared to encounter and make the most of opportunities like those described. To some extent every angler makes his own luck – by thinking things out, having confidence in his approach and, above all, putting in plenty of time. Then, sooner or later, things come right – and the result is a red-letter day. In this book we have tried to help with the planning and confidence aspects; it is up to you to make the effort. Anyone who is willing to adopt a single-minded attitude can still catch big bass, even in these days of nylon gill nets and high prices.

The days which we have chosen to describe are not those on which we caught our biggest ever fish. If they have any common feature it is the fact that we each used our experience to decide where, when and how to fish and, for once, the bass agreed with us. Anyway that's enough of the preliminaries so let's get down to the beach – with Alan first.

I was on holiday and it was a brilliant July day. I had caught a few fish during the week and, as I sat in the pub at lunch time, taking my time over the ploughman's and cold beer, I looked forward to fishing that afternoon. I had travelled thirty miles to enable my wife to meet some old friends and whilst they were chatting, making up for lost time, my thoughts were on the bass that I hoped to catch. So far I had done everything possible to ensure success: I had a bucket well filled with large peeler and soft edible crabs, the chafed line had been replaced and my hooks were honed to razor sharpness, there were plenty of leads in the bag and all I needed was co-operation from the fish.

Two hours before low water I made my way down to the beach and walked about two hundred yards to where the current just offshore was forced to speed up as it raced over a shallow rocky ledge, well covered by kelp. After baiting up with a large soft crab, I cast out about thirty-five yards to an area just uptide of the ledge. Holding the rod with intense concentration, feeling every tiny movement of weed and water through the line, I was ready for the fish to arrive. Fifteen minutes later I rebaited and the procedure was repeated with no sign of a bite until low water, when I began to think that the day would be a blank.

The fish usually arrived on this mark before low tide and, as I stood sweating in the afternoon sun, I began to look at the distractions on the beach. A few shore crabs were fighting in the water's edge over my discarded bait, and, a short distance from where I stood, a small boy was turning over rocks. As the boy approached I could see that he had a good-sized edible crab in his hand. He smiled, held out the crab and said, 'Want a softy, Mister?' He was not fishing himself so I gratefully accepted and was about to reel in, to bait up again, when a slight but distinctive pluck signified a bite. I immediately gave a yard of slack line and

A dream come true – bass of 10½ and 9½lb.

waited. There was a twitching sensation and the line began to tighten, faster and more positively than the tightness caused by the current. I struck hard and took a couple of steps backwards, striking again.

The rod bent well over into what was obviously a good fish. On a beach rod and tackle there is seldom need to give much line to a bass, but this one was pulling very hard and my fingers fumbled to loosen the clutch as I was dragged towards the water. The fish swam out into the strong current and fought deep (in my experience a common characteristic of big bass); for several minutes I anxiously held on, hoping that the line would not fray and break on the rough submerged rocks. The fish then surfaced and I saw a large mouth, wide open and shaking violently. The bass went down again and I allowed it to move up against the current, hopefully tiring itself. After a short while I pumped the bass in to the shore and, when it lay grounded on the wet wrack at my feet, I lifted it up by the gill cover and heaved it up the beach. This fish was about two and a half feet long, it looked to be the biggest bass I had yet caught. I killed it quickly.

Shaking with excitement, I became aware of the boy, who was

Another dream – not one under 8lb and all caught on plugs.

staring at the fish, wide-eyed. Having learned from experience to strike while the iron is hot, I quickly baited up and cast out again. The whole procedure was repeated; I had a bite which, this time, was simply a hard pull. A firm strike resulted in another good fish hooked. This time I didn't see the bass at all until it was being landed, but it was not much smaller than the first one.

I killed this fish also and, amazed at catching two bass of this size, I recast. Several casts and three-quarters of an hour later I caught a third fish of slightly smaller size; on the spring balance this one scaled a little over 8lb. I returned the fish to the sea and, as it swam away, the boy could contain himself no longer and asked bluntly why on earth I had put it back. I explained that I was on holiday, and since I could only make use of two fish there was no point taking any more. He was obviously upset and at first I could not understand why. Then I remembered the crab he had given me – perhaps it had caught that last fish. Feeling a little guilty I promised him that if I caught another he could have it.

By this time I was prepared to experiment. It had been my intention for some time to try live fish baits, so I put on a 6/0 hook and three butterfish, each hooked once through the root of the tail. I hoped for an even bigger fish as the bait was cast out into the current, which was now fierce.

Almost immediately the butterfish were taken with a strong pull, but the strike met with only light resistance. I was able to reel in the bass easily, a fish of 3½lb, and I gave it to the boy. His eyes lit up and he was obviously thrilled; in fact he then collected some more crabs for me before taking his fish home.

Shortly after my companion left the scene I beached my fifth fish, a bass of 5½lb, which was returned after weighing. That was the last bite of the day. In the space of two hours I had caught five bass of 3½lb, 5½lb, 8lb, 9½lb and 10½lb.

I had previously landed more bass in a session but, as I drove home, it occurred to me that this day had been special. It had been my recurring daydream that I might catch bass of 8lb, 9lb and 10lb in a single trip; now, at last, I had done it, with two other fish as a bonus.

That ten-pounder was also the first of my double-figure bass and the occasion is still very clear in my memory. There were several features of that day which, in the light of my present experience, are characteristic of exceptionally good fishing days: the size of the tide, the particular tide in the series, the sight of fish moving earlier in the day, and the settled but occasionally breezy weather. All were good omens, as I now realise. I have, since that day, caught many bass but I still think of it as the day my dream came true.

And now down to a different shore, this time with Mike.

The build-up to my best ever day (in fact days) of bass fishing began in November of the previous year (1982). It was a week of spring tides and by getting down to the shore after a late lunch it was possible to fish the tide up. Dave Cooling, Richard (my son) and I had arranged to go fishing on the Saturday afternoon, so when I saw the weather forecast on the TV on Friday evening I was a bit peeved. The chart was covered in lines; there were so many that it looked like a spider's web. I cursed the smiling face of the weather man – obviously he was not going fishing on the following day.

For once the predictions turned out to be spot on and the wind, which kept me awake all Friday night, was still blowing as I dragged myself out of bed on Saturday. Throughout the morning it increased in intensity and by the time Dave's car drew up to collect us it was a howling force 9. Perhaps it wouldn't be so bad along the coast, we said optimistically, but in our heart of hearts we could see the writing on the wall.

As we tramped along the shore, the waves were crashing against the rocks, half way up the slope of the beach, in a threatening fashion. We decided to fish the most sheltered cove we could find and, after tackling up, we cast our baits of worm and squid into the rolling swell and settled down to wait. Following the statutory half-hour without a bite, Richard became restless, as usual. 'I'm going out there to have a go,' he said, pointing to the rocky headland. My reply was as he expected: 'You certainly are not!' 'I'll be careful, Dad' was his response, and, before I could say anything else, he was on his way. I had only time to shout after him 'Come back before the tide cuts you off!' before he was out of earshot.

From our relatively comfortable pitch Dave and I could see the tiny figure outlined against a permanent background of white, foaming surf. From where we stood it looked unfishable, but the figure scurried about with such a purposeful air that we began to wonder what he was playing at. After about twenty minutes, just as I was beginning to cast worried looks at the incoming tide, we saw Richard turn in our direction and begin to make his way towards us along the rocks. We exchanged knowing looks – of course we, older and wiser, had known it would be too rough for him to fish – but as he approached we could see that his left hand was hidden by long silvery-white shapes, which quickly showed themselves to be two fine bass of about 5lb each. The plug dangling from his rod tip showed the successful method. We were green with envy.

On the following day, with the wind still blowing, I confirmed these events by taking seven bass averaging 5½lb in less than an hour from Richard's ledge by using a similar 4½-inch floating, jointed plug. All through the following winter we chafed impatiently at the bit, even more than usually keen for the start of the next season and the first fierce pull to show that the bass were in.

On a Thursday in early June Dave went down one evening, on his own, to fish Richard's mark of the previous autumn. The tide was coming in and there was a moderate sea, but in an entire evening's fishing he had no bites. The only significant feature had been a large bass which moved behind his Rebel plug as it was retrieved from the deep water. He related the experience to me by telephone and, the following evening, we were out there again. The wind was getting up a bit now and three of us – Dave, Martin Williams and myself – fished assiduously with the wind at our backs into the deep water surging along the side of the rocky ledge. It was to be Martin's evening: he had four takes on his Rebel plug and landed them all. They ranged from 7½lb to 9½lb. I had two bites, fishing by his side. One produced a wrasse of about 1½lb, the other came unstuck. Dave, also fishing alongside, had nothing.

We returned home well pleased with the evening's sport. Martin, as might be expected, was like a cat with two tails. We dropped him off at his digs (he was a student) and then Dave took me home. As we unloaded the gear from the car, I said, 'How about a try tomorrow morning?' 'OK,' came the reply, 'What time?' 'I'll pick you up about 4.30,' I said. If Dave blanched at the thought of only four hours sleep it did not show, so the trip was on.

The night was still black outside as I dressed, scalded my mouth with a cup of coffee, picked up the rod, reel and box of lures and set off to collect my fellow early-bird. As always he was waiting at the door when I arrived and, within seconds, we were on our way.

Down on the seashore the wind of the previous evening had dropped but a heavy swell was still running and the brisk surf was pounding across the flat rocky ledge. We began by fishing into the deeper water where Martin had, on the previous evening, caught his bass, but after half an hour we had not registered any sign of interest from the fish. We changed our lures once or twice but without effect. The early morning sun was already shining from a cloudless blue sky, promising a superb day ahead. I was using a tiny silver Toby spoon now and mentioned to Dave that I was going to try a few casts into the shallow water. There had been nothing in the deep water of the gully so it was more with hope than expectation that I retreated on to the ledge.

I waded out up to my knees into the sparkling, boiling surf to give myself a few extra yards of distance with the small lure. On the first retrieve the rod tip knocked and I thought for an instant that it was the pull of a fish, but decided that the lure must have touched a rocky ridge on the way in. The second cast was fished out uneventfully until the powerful longshore current had swept the Toby inshore of where I was standing. The water was as clear as crystal and I could see the little metal leaf glinting as I raised the rod to complete the retrieve. Suddenly there was an explosive take and a bass was hooked. It fought gamely on the 8lb line, but since it only weighed 1½lb it was quickly brought to hand, unhooked and returned.

I shouted above the rushing of the surf to let Dave know of my success. After I had returned the fish I immediately changed the lure for a larger one, a J11 Rapala, and cast again. The plug landed twenty yards out in the seething waves and, as it hit the water, it was seized violently. The clutch whined and line was torn from the spool with great speed and power, making full use of the strong current and the surging undertow. Dave appeared at my side as I slid my catch on to the flat, wet rocks, an event which we repeated no less than forty-seven times in the next two hours. Every fish seemed to bite more fiercely and to fight with more verve than the one before. When we stopped fishing it was the result of having caught enough, not because the fish had gone – almost a unique event in my experience.

As they were landed the bass often coughed up bundles of little sandeels. At times, as we fished, we could see bass breaking the surface in groups of half a dozen together. A lure flicked into the midst of such a group invariably produced a good bite and, usually, a hooked fish. Very few bass were missed or lost.

Inevitably, on the following Sunday morning I was down on the ledge again, this time accompanied by Martin. The events of the previous day were repeated, with the exception that conditions, if anything, were even better. This time our total, in two hours, was fifty-two fish with an average weight of nearly 6lb and the biggest (the only one I kept) 9½lb. My personal tally was fifty-eight fish in the two short sessions. I hope that one day I may do better.

13
Still Hooked on Bass!

...for too long we have been killing far too many bass.

Don Kelley, *Forty Anglers*, 1994

ML   BASSING IN THE TWENTY-FIRST CENTURY

Life History

Since the first edition of this book there have been a number of strong year classes. The 1976 fish were abundant. They suffered badly from commercial fishing when they were just 'takeable' but featured strongly in the stocks for many years afterwards (well into the 1990s). Other particularly strong year classes were 1981 and 1982, both of which should still be represented as the specimen fish of today (2002). Also good was 1989 and many of the fish now weighing six or seven pounds appear to be from that year's young. The 1990s have also produced several strong year groups, some of which probably suffered badly from the effects of a cold spell in the 1996–97 winter, but it looks as if the 1997 and 1998 fish are very abundant.

The increase in minimum landing size to 36cm (it should, of course, be much more!) and the introduction of bass nursery areas (*partly* protected from commercial fishing) in 1990 may well be helping the young fish in their first few years of life and promoting heavy recruitment of 'school bass' to the stocks. Conversely, the effects of pair trawling in the western approaches and heavy gill-netting inshore are still depleting the numbers of larger fish.

These latter effects have combined to dramatically reduce the average size of bass in some areas. It would be a pity if the bass anglers of the future were to think that a one-and-a-half pound bass is the norm. Equally, by shifting our methods to the use of fly gear and small baits or lures to improve sport with these small fish we may unwittingly give the impression (to the powers that be) that

191

we are satisfied with large catches of little bass. This is far from being the case. What is really required is a balanced stock of bass that includes enough decent sized fish to give anglers a real chance to catch a 'specimen' now and again.

Lines

Since this book was first written, braided lines have become very popular. These lines are excellent for spinning. They are very strong in relation to their diameter and so they improve casting distances and reduce water resistance. They do however need special knots, for example the Palomar knot for attaching hooks or swivels and the Albright knot for a direct join between braid and nylon (the latter must be snugged up *really* tight to avoid sub-sequent breakage). If in doubt join braid to nylon by a small swivel or a clip.

Since braided lines are opaque some anglers still prefer a trace of nylon or fluorocarbon between line and lure (I do this although I have no evidence that it matters). Some of the fusion-type braids such as Fireline have a coating that tends to fray and to go 'furry' after a few sessions. This furriness does not seem to weaken the line but can make the line sticky on the first cast or two of every trip. Other, non-coated, braids like Whiplash easily separate into the individual filaments. They are just as strong and much more supple but in my view are a bit more susceptible to damage by hook points and barbs. It is difficult to detect damage in any braided line so you should cut off any sections with frayed or broken filaments. Elsewhere in my original sections of this book you can effectively substitute 'twenty-pound braid' for 'eight-pound nylon'.

Spinning

The methods described in the first edition of this book are as good today as they always were. Big natural baits will still tempt the largest fish and buoyant plug baits are always likely to attract and catch many bass. However, it would be a dull world if there were never any changes and, at least in terms of artificial baits, there have been some definite improvements in tackle and two or three worthwhile additions to the lure box.

Although bass are often very close inshore there are times when

Alan unhooking a 6/0 from the mouth of a big Dorset bass

they can be frustratingly just out of range. There are few things more annoying than to see good fish, as they feed on fry, breaking the surface eighty yards out. Try as you might it may be impossible to cast even a large balsa or plastic minnow anywhere near the feeding zone. What do you do?

Of course it is always possible to clip on a heavy Toby or metal jig and hurl it out to the bass. Indeed this can be an effective ploy, but the fish are not always keen on fast retrieved metal, the water may be shallow out there and the bottom is just as likely to be snag-ridden, so it is fortunate that there are good alternatives.

One of the more interesting developments is the 'Bass Bullet'. These are spindle-shaped streamlined slivers of wood, heavily weighted internally so that they cast enormous distances. Despite their high density the profile of the lures makes them swim near the surface even on a slow retrieve. The bullets have very little intrinsic *action* apart from a slow sinuous wiggle but it is possible to give them more movement by working them with the rod. In many ways they are similar to the 'jerkbaits' mentioned by Alan.

193

Bass Bullets are coated with a thin layer of opalescent plastic, coloured blue or green on one side and pearly white on the other. They come in several sizes and a couple of different profiles but all cast well and fish shallow. One apparent drawback is that the 'Bullets' are armed only with a single tail treble. This might be regarded as a big disadvantage for fish which normally take their prey from the side but the proof of the lure is in the catching and there is no doubt that they can, at times, be excellent fish catchers. My pal Nigel Thorne, using Bass Bullets (which were new to him at the time!), seriously outfished my plugs on a couple of occasions. Of course, these lures do sink quickly on a slack line and as such are liable to be lost in snags unless you remain in constant contact with them.

Another option when the fish are at distance is the countdown plug. These resemble normal 'floaters' in shape and size but cast substantially further (but not as far as Bass Bullets or Chug Bugs) and can be fished at different depths. For two whole seasons I used Rapala countdowns as my standard plugs and caught well over a hundred bass in each season. Some of these fish would not have been caught on buoyant lures because they would have been out of range.

Countdowns are useful when fish are taking quite small food items (fry) because it is possible to achieve the required distance with a relatively small lure. They sink slowly and, as the name suggests, tend to 'hold' the depth at which you begin your retrieve. On the down side, the action is less vigorous than that of a buoyant plug of similar dimensions and *they will not float free* if they encounter a snag. The bigger versions, such as the Rapala J-11 seem to have more action than their smaller relatives.

The third and perhaps the most useful innovation is the popping plug. These chunky, more or less conical, plastic lures are floaters. They are heavy, often containing ball bearings or other weights to assist casting (and to rattle when the lure is chugged!). Nevertheless they are still low-density lures that float on the water surface. They are very bulky for their length. In fact I have often described them as 'sticks of rock', nevertheless poppers can be incredibly efficient bass catchers. One of the first surface popper designs introduced to use by Steve Butler and his pal Mike Hughes, fishing in North Wales, was the 'Chug Bug'. The 'Bug' is a shiny, blue and silver lure about 11cm in length (15cm including the big, decorated, tail treble) and 2.5cm in thickness at the front end. These lures cast almost as well as Bass Bullets but they float high in the water with the tail end hanging down beneath the surface.

Poppers need to be worked by the angler either by jerking the rod or by reeling in sharply. The Americans (who have much more experience of these lures) suggest that it is a mistake to use the rod to impart action and that it may be best to point the rod at the lure and use the reel to move the popper. On a steady retrieve they will plough along the water surface generating a bit of a bow wave and a wake. However, to get the best results they need more effort from the angler. Perhaps the best way to describe popper fishing is to give a short account of the first time I used them.

Alan had joined me for an early September evening's fishing on the Dorset coast. I knew that a particular spot had been producing lots of bass to flies and plugs over the past two or three days. When we arrived on the shore – a mass of cobbles, shingle and boulders – the sea was pretty choppy and considerably rougher than of late. A couple of other anglers were already fishing, casting and retrieving Thundersticks and Bombers. I clipped on my favourite J-11 buoyant Rapala and Alan, freshly enthusiastic from a recent trip to Wales with Steve Butler, attached a large Saltwater Chug Bug. We were both using longish spinning rods and had fixed-spool reels loaded with Fireline braid, which has little or no stretch.

It was not long before I had a take on the Rapala and landed a small bass of perhaps two pounds. I must admit that, at this point, I was feeling slightly smug about catching the first fish on the old, reliable lure. However, it was not long until Alan gave a shout and I saw that his rod was bent into a fish. He soon played and landed his catch, which proved to be similar in size to the one I had caught. There were obviously lots of small bass about and I thought it was the ideal chance to try 'bugging' for myself. Alan kindly loaned me (in fact gave me) a lure, the same as his own, and I quickly removed the Rapala and clipped it on.

The first impression was one of easy casting as the bug soared out to sea. The cast had to be smooth to avoid the lure tumbling in the air and fouling the line but it was not much of a problem. The second thing I noticed was that the lure needed to be left for a few seconds, to allow the line to settle onto the surface, after the cast. An instant jerk on the rod would make the lure skid across the surface and again there was a possibility of fouling the line. I

The stomach of a three-pounder, the food that was in it and the lure that caught the fish.

watched Alan's technique. Chug, wait, chug, wait, and tried to copy what he was doing. By now he was into a second fish and I had not had a sniff. Confidence quickly ebbs away in these circumstances but I knew that the fish were there so out went the lure again.

Cast and chug it back in, cast and chug it back in, cast for a third time, chug, pause, chug, pause. I watched carefully as each chug caused water to spray up from the dished front of the lure. The bug was almost back to the edge now and I shortened my sweep of the rod to avoid flipping it out of the water. I was waiting for it to drop into a trough between waves for each chug and then tightening to it with a couple of turns of the reel. I turned my head towards Alan as I wound the handle and as I did so I felt the rod pull over to the weight of a fish. I was amazed. The bass had taken the lure, as it lay, more or less motionless, between chugs. I have since found that this is a common time for a take but, despite knowing this, every time it happens it is a complete surprise to me.

The fish seem almost to hook themselves. Whether this would be the case with stretchy nylon lines, as opposed to braid, I don't know. In any case it is well worth having half-a-metre or so of nylon between the braid and the lure. This is not so much to reduce visibility as to prevent tangling or damage to the braid should the lure double back on itself in flight or when you are retrieving (a frequent event with inexperienced chuggers).

It is not easily possible to tell just how much the 'next chug' is responsible for setting the hook firmly after a bite. The fact that the bass take these lures, as they lie stationary on the surface, suggests that a closer resemblance to a baitfish might be even more effective. It would, presumably, be possible to rig a small dead fish (sand smelt, sprat, pouting or the like) with a cork or button at its head to combine the attraction of a surface popper with the appearance and smell/taste of the real thing. Of course it is always a compromise between time spent baiting up, durability of the bait or lure and attractiveness to the fish and so on, and it is likely that, at times, the artificial would out-fish the bait and vice versa.

Anyway, here is the basic method just as Steve told me:

Hi Mike,

Over the years Mike Hughes and myself have been using the Chug bug in a variety of different waters and conditions around the North Wales coast, from calm to slight seas, slight to semi-rough seas and in strong tidal waters. When we have a choice we tend to prefer the calm to slight water to any other.

HOW TO USE THE BUG

After you have cast your lure out, start jerking your rod to make your bug cause as much commotion on the surface of the water as possible for five to ten seconds. This action will get the attention of any Bass that are in the vicinity. Leave your lure motionless for around five seconds, then start working it with small twitches for about a third of the retrieve, then leave motionless for five seconds. Next jerk your rod violently again to cause commotion on the surface with the lure for another five to ten seconds then leave again for five seconds, then again bring the lure in with small twitches for another third of the retrieve, then repeat as above. As your lure comes within 10ft of the shoreline, don't lift the lure out of the water; leave it motionless for another five seconds as Bass can

Dorset bass of 8, 9 and 10lb caught by Mike and Alan on crab.

attack at any time. I have had quite a few Bass take the lure at this time.

From when you first cast out keep your eyes peeled. Look out for swirls and boils around your lure. Try to distinguish between the boil a fish would make and the swirl around a rock; always be on alert.

The golden rule when using surface lures for Bass is '*Don't strike as soon as you have an attack from a fish*' let the fish take the lure. The best time to strike is when your line starts to tighten up, when you can feel the pull of the fish or if your lure disappears from sight for a few seconds, then, strike hard. If you miss the attack, don't bring in your lure, leave it out there then work it with very fine twitches, this should entice the fish to attack again.

A couple of tips.

When jerking your rod to work your lure try to reel in your slack line at the same time. If you don't your line will sometimes tangle around the front treble, this then makes it hard to work the lure correctly. Also change your hooks to a finer wire; I tend to go for size 2 trebles.

I hope this is of some help – Steve.

In a second e-mail, when I asked him about the season for 'popping', Steve added a couple of extra comments:

I don't usually start my Bass lure fishing until the beginning of May; it all depends on the weather. If there is snow on the hills in April the fishing starts off slow. So the answer is May with the popper. As the temperature of the water goes up they are more active. We found near the end of the Bass season they didn't hit the popper as aggressively as they did in August, September and the first few weeks in October. It may be the same in these early months, down to the temperature of the water. The water on your coast is warmer at this time of year than ours, so it may be worth you carrying on trying the Bug.

All the best – Steve

There may still be a lot to learn about using these surface baits. Some other B.A.S.S. members are already experimenting (apparently with some degree of success) with methods to enhance the attraction of poppers. Steady retrieves and constant but uneven working of the lure appear to be very effective in some circumstances. My own thoughts are that any method of making an essentially static bait look or smell more fishlike is well worth a try.

Fly Fishing

For a long time anglers in the USA have been using fly tackle in saltwater, particularly in the tropics. The vast range of predatory species available to fishermen in the Caribbean, off Florida and along the Pacific coast has encouraged the growth of this sport. Very often big game fish are the quarry, so the tackle used is quite heavy and the flies are so big that they could not be cast with ease on conventional trout rods. However, these days the use of fly gear in the seas around Britain is becoming increasingly popular. Indeed, there are already books written on the subject. As might be expected much of the information is simply lifted from the American literature, but there is a small but growing body of anglers who are very knowledgeable about fly fishing for sea fish and, in particular, for bass. For the experienced specialist it may be worth investing in expensive gear but, in practice, many bass (and mullet, scad, mackerel, pollack, coalfish, garfish and even wrasse) can be caught on relatively cheap fly gear.

My friends and I have been catching lots of bass on flies since the 1970s (see Operation Sea Angler on http//:www.mikeladle.com). In fact quite a lot of large bass were taken on both mullet flies (artificial maggots) and salmon streamers and tubes in those days. My own tackle (no criterion of perfection) is simply a nine-foot 'trout' fly rod designed to cast a number 6 or 7 line. A cheap reel big enough to hold the fly line and fifty metres of strong nylon backing, a weight-forward floating fly line and a spool of 6lb BS nylon for casts have caught me a lot of bass.

Nowadays modern flies imitating small fish are particularly popular with bassing experts. One of the favourites, the Clouser Minnow, is tied to fish with the hook point uppermost, allowing the fly to be drawn through and over heavy weed growth without too much risk of snagging. Myself, I often use the smaller sizes of Delta eel or thin strips of mackerel in lieu of a tied fly and find that they are extremely effective. In 2001 several fellow members of B.A.S.S., all of whom are keen fly fishermen, began to make serious efforts to catch bass on fly gear.

Geoff Hancock who has caught huge numbers of sea fish on flies gave me the following tips:

A fishing benefit provided by using 'the fly'

Sometimes fly-fishing can provide exceptional representation of natural food items because the lures are relatively lightweight with 'in-built' action.

Factors important to life-like presentation are:
- The design of the fly (weight, type and proportions of materials).
- The type of fly line and leader construction employed.
- The stripping technique.

This fish took a Redgill. The dark shadow of the barrel lead which provides casting weight is just visible through the body of the lure

- The water conditions (current, turbulence, wave action and so on).

Examples:

1) Use of Sandeel Pattern

During observation of the escape behaviour of sandeels (Cape Cod, USA), whilst standing amongst them as they were being chased by striped bass, I have noticed that the eels often dodge attacks by fleeing downwards, or occasionally upwards, rather than sideways within the water column.

I often fish the North Wales coast using 6-inch sand eel pattern flies that have a weighted head with the hook point riding uppermost when being retrieved. Using a floating line, these flies can be made to jerk vertically by employing a series of sharp pulls during stripping. A sudden change in vertical direction of the fly causes it to 'hinge' along its body providing an attractive flight reaction. This technique has worked well in water with little current when the fly is brought back to the rod and in a strong current when the fly travels with the current or is held against the current.

201

2) Use of Currents

When fishing strong currents close to or over ledges or other structures I have had some success by making use of the current to sweep
the fly into, or over, an area where the fish are likely to be waiting.
For example, this technique can be employed when fishing ledges
that run perpendicular to the shore and over which the water tends
to run more quickly than on either side [prime bass spots as we
know: ML].

Using an intermediate or floating line, the fly is cast up-current
of the ledge and by mending line or holding the rod tip to either
side, the fly can be made to swing round onto the ledge or alternatively off the opposite side. The line suddenly stopping within its
normal path usually indicates a take.

In some instances variations in the current push the line faster
than the fly, causing it to form a bow. As the line reaches the end
of its swing the bow straightens as the fly sweeps in an arc and lifts
within the water column. Again this upward movement of the fly
seems particularly attractive to fish and by holding the rod tip
at angles to the line, the fly can be made to rise in the water at
the point of the fish-holding structure. The weight of the fly is
important in this technique and should be adjusted to suit the
speed of the current.

Geoff

Fly-fishing for bass can be a very rewarding and satisfying way to
catch. You are not just limited to the schoolies either, as some
would have you believe. In the right conditions with the right fly,
anything can happen. One morning things fell into place for fellow
B.A.S.S. member Steve Binke. Steve and his pal Darren Roberts
were fishing, at dawn, from a West Sussex beach. Steve was using
a 9ft, #8 Sage fly rod. Darren had decided to stick with his spinning rod. Both were wearing chest waders. There was a cool
south-westerly of around ten knots, pushing nicely onto the beach.
This was, as Steve put it:

. . . a good start, as this will normally bring the bass within range
of a fly rod. There was good cloud cover, so light levels would stay
low giving us more fishing time. Line was a clear intermediate

A fish of five-and-a-half pounds that took a streamer fly, fished on fly tackle.

shooting head; 9ft tapered leader, with an 8lb point. My choice of flies that morning was all based on an American pattern called the Clouser deep minnow, in a variety of colours.

After a couple of fishless hours Steve decided to move along to a set of breakwaters. This is what happened:

I arrived at the first of a set of breakwaters, making a few casts alongside. Cast out; count the line down and strip it back in. The amount of time you allow the line to sink before commencing a retrieve, will dictate how deep your fly will fish in the water. This makes an intermediate line a good choice in relatively shallow water of less than ten feet. Any deeper and a fast sinking line would be more useful, and quicker! I had reached the third set of break-waters and nearly completed another retrieve. Rather than draw the shooting head right in, I leave around ten feet outside the top ring to help with the next cast. What I do is to move the rod tip up and to one side so as to do a roll cast, but also to check the fly, as it comes into view, for any weed, etc. It was whilst doing this that I saw a bass of around four pounds follow my fly right into the edge of the surf, not more than six feet away. The bass saw me and with a flick of its tail was gone.

This was just what I needed and I fished on with renewed enthusiasm. But as with all things fishy nothing happens when you expect it to. After another ten minutes of casting and stripping my mind had started to wander again, this time to cups of warm tea and cake. I looked up to where Darren was, only to see him pouring something hot from a flask. Now I was really torn as I desperately wanted a cuppa, but also to keep fishing and just where had he been hiding that flask all morning!

Suddenly the line between my fingers snapped tight as an unseen force hit the fly. I strip-struck a couple of times to really send home the hook, then raised the rod high. The fish turned and made out to sea, normally I can stop a fish pretty quickly after a hook-up but this one kept on going and going – forty – fifty yards before it began to slow. I shot a quick glance to where Darren was, to see him running down the beach towards me. 'Is it a good size?' he asked. The next moment the bass hit the surface for all to see. There was no mistaking, this fish was huge, and we were both a bit speechless. It seemed like an age that the fish just lay on the surface fifty yards out, and then it gave a kick and was off again.

By this stage I had managed to regain some composure. The fish was directly onto the reel so I could give or retrieve line in a normal fashion. For the second time it hit the surface and just lay there, this scared the life out of me as it really puts the hook hold under strain. I didn't want to put too much pressure on, but the fish would not move. In the end I had to walk up the beach very slowly drawing the fish nearer. Eventually I had it under control, I was back in the surf with the bass plodding around in front of me at about ten yards range. My arm was starting to ache by now as I desperately tried to bring the bass in on a wave. Three attempts later and the fish was mine. It looked even bigger out of the water, and at nine-pounds-two-ounces it was my largest ever bass. A few photos were taken before returning her to the sea.

Now to sort out the post-catch chaos. Darren had already started to cast his lure in the general direction and rightly so as there were likely to be more fish about. I checked my watch to see where on the tide I had caught. Three hours down from flood. Quickly I set about changing the fly as the fish had really mangled the blue/white Clouser. The only other fly I had big enough was an orange/white Clouser tied on a size 2 stainless hook. A quick roll cast put the line out around twenty feet. I used the water's surface to load the rod as I hauled the line off. I shot another fifteen feet on the back-cast, and then hauled the line again on the forward cast. Minimum effort, maximum distance. This went out around thirty-five yards. A count of ten seconds allowed it to sink and I began the retrieve.

Third strip and the line stopped dead as another big fish hit the fly. My friend looked on in disbelief as he had been fishing a lure all around the area for the past ten minutes without a touch. This fish also made a long run out to sea taking forty yards of line before stopping. I could feel its head shaking in a bid to rid itself of the offending item it had just eaten. I started to apply some pressure, but the bass was having none of it and made another run of around twenty yards. I had wound the drag up on the reel in a bid to slow the fish down and it seemed to be working. Just when I thought I was beginning to get things under control, the hook pulled. My heart missed a beat and that horrible feeling washed over me that only losing a good fish does to you. Although we fished on for another couple of hours, the big fish, it seemed, had moved out with the tide leaving us to chase the 12-inch schoolies. I have been back to this mark many times but never repeated that morning's fishing, not yet anyway! Its days like these that keep you coming back, just in case.

Cheers, Steve

AV BRINGING THINGS UP TO DATE

Locality

The first edition of this book was written while I was living in South Wales, but since moving to Devon in 1988, I have had the challenge of gaining vital local knowledge again. During the last twelve years or so I have done less bottom fishing and used lures of various sorts and prawns as a means of exploring new shores. However, it is interesting to note that, with the exception of a 9lb-plus fish on a plug, my biggest Devon bass have all been taken on bottom-fished bait.

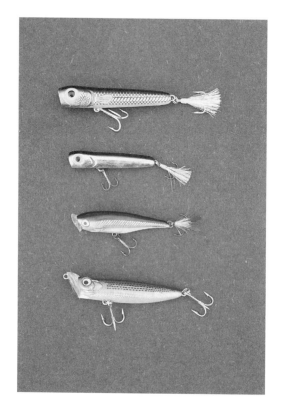

Surface lures. Two Chug Bugs, a Skitterpop and a Chico Boca: all of them cast well and catch bass.

Prawns

After moving to south Devon, I spent a couple of years using live prawns most of the time and found that, in this way, it was relatively easy to catch Devonian bass during the daylight. The drawback was always the attention prawns attract from the huge numbers of wrasse present. To avoid this, it is best to try to catch the fish in midwater or above and accept that prawns fished near rocks will catch the wrasse that swim up the vertical faces. It is helpful to use a non-stretch braid for float fishing and for prawn fishing. It is important to remember that the strike needs to be delayed for several seconds so that the bass has time to position the prawn correctly for swallowing. If, when the float goes under, the line is reeled in until resistance is felt, which usually takes about three to five seconds, a strike can be successfully made; once a bass has taken a prawn then, as long as the float is only a small one, the prawn is unlikely to be rejected.

For prawn fishing I usually use Fireline braid mainline and ¼ oz lead with an appropriately sized float (a small one). I use a trace of 1–2 metres made of 8lb mono and hooks of size 2 to 1/0 depending on prawn size. Incidentally, although I have tried fluorocarbon for prawn traces I found it rather stiff with low knot strength. Consequently I now use ordinary clear mono of a reliable brand.

The clear South Devon water often meant that I would have the experience of catching a fish quite quickly and then have to wait a long time, or move elsewhere, since the commotion of landing a fish would put off the bass for a while. In roughish water, in the rain and on dull days, this problem was less likely.

During these experimental years I caught a few fish approaching five pounds on prawns but took bigger fish on lures and bottom-fished baits. On one occasion I had fished for a couple of hours using prawns and taken three bass and more wrasse. Then a shoal of big bass turned up, feeding on smaller bait fish. They were just out of usual plug-casting range, but the large swirls, with heads followed by big tails were a grand sight. I quickly changed over to a J-13 Rapala, which casts quite well, and, after several casts, hooked and landed a bass of 5lb-plus. Shortly afterwards I hooked another bass, which took quite a time to subdue. I was just about to net this fish, which was more than twice the size of the previous one, when the plug popped out. As it swam away I could have wept. As I said before, I think that prawns are excellent baits but I prefer other methods for the bigger fish.

Sandeels

Since moving to south Devon I have used live sandeels from the shore and found them to be very effective (bass up to 8lb), particularly when legered at night on my local beaches. When using this bait in calm conditions I have found that bass takes are often cautious, which surprised me. I have used light (1–2oz) leads and a 3–4ft trace with a 2/0–4/0 hook depending on the eel size. For casting from the shore, the best way to hook a live eel is to pass the hook through both eye sockets; the eel withstands a cast of up to fifty yards and remains alive to swim around. It is best to use a hook with a reasonably large barb when using this method otherwise the eels often manage to escape from the hook.

Looking After Live Prawns and Sandeels

It is well worth the trouble needed to keep a store of some of the best live baits readily available.

Prawns are the easiest to keep. Any fish tank can be used, but it needs to be kept cool and dark. My tank is about 4 cubic feet in volume and I use a power head with sub-gravel filter to aerate it. There is gravel at the bottom and I find that prawns live well in this tank. They need to be fed, now and again, or else they will eat each other. Dead prawns must be removed every day or you may find yourself with a tank of dead prawns and polluted water that must be completely changed. A dozen prawns survive in a small plastic bucket for at least an hour without aeration, and regular changing of water at the venue keeps them in perfect condition.

Sandeels are a bit more difficult to look after. They need to be in a well-aerated tank with fine gravel (about lentil sized) to burrow into. It is not feasible to feed them (they eat plankton) and they must be inspected regularly to remove eels that may die under the gravel. Eels in a bucket must be aerated in transit to or from fishing and then water needs to be changed regularly or constantly aerated at the venue. Some anglers successfully transport prawns and sandeels amongst hessian sacking dampened with seawater; this method is more reliable if the hessian is kept cool by placing freezer packs or containers of ice underneath. A small net with a fine mesh, such as those sold for aquaria, is needed to extract the prawns or eels from your tank (and you will have lots of fun catching the eels that jump out of the tank).

Mackerel Heads

For some reason, one of the best, perhaps the best part of a fish for bass bait is the head, especially if it has the guts attached.

Several anglers I have met think that the best bottom-fished bait is mackerel head. I have had a number of experiences that back up this idea. When fishing in South Wales on sandy beaches, I caught large bass on big mackerel baits, including a number on heads.

One summer when I was on a North Wales holiday, my brother-in-law Phil (picture front cover) came home from a mackerel fishing session to report that, having got bored with catching mackerel, he had put a mackerel head on a 5/0 hook and free-lined

A bass caught on a Skitterpop lure. Note that the fish is hooked on the mid-body hook.

it on his mackerel line. To summarise the session, he hooked three big fish on heads, but was broken by each one. The following day we were both at Phil's venue and, as the evening progressed, we both free-lined mackerel heads on heavier line. This time there was only one run, to Phil, and eventually I netted a bass of well over ten pounds for him.

I suggest that if you want to catch a big bass, and the mackerel have been feeding well, it is a good idea to bait up with a head as the light goes. It seems logical to suppose that bass, especially big ones, are attracted to feeding mackerel and are in the vicinity to be tempted. Heads have the added benefit of withstanding crab activity for longer than the rest of the body.

Hooks

Since the first edition of this book there have been great improvements in hook design and manufacture. The hooks I used to favour, namely Mustad 79510, 79515 and 7780C remain available and are still good bass hooks; indeed they seem better now since the points are finer and sharper. However, there are now many other good hooks on the market, a lot of them with chemically sharpened points, which removes the need to sharpen them first before fishing. A few of the new hooks are brittle, but most are very good; even the Cox and Rawle 'Meat-hook' is sharp enough to be struck into a hard bass mouth. However, it is still necessary to check hook points regularly and resharpen when the point becomes dull or turned, which is a frequent event when fishing over rough ground.

More and more lures of the plug type have now found their way onto the British market, many of them having a remarkably life-like finish, which has to be a good thing. However, such lures are often supplied with hooks that are not the best, being heavy and thick in the wire with long points and large barbs. Others, particularly those with a bright chrome finish, I have found liable to snap. As a result I often change the hooks supplied for better ones; I use Gamakatsu or Owner brand.

Lines

Mike and I have both mentioned the recent introduction and advantages of modern braided lines that have little or no stretch (although some of them do have a tendency to snap under sudden pressure, for example on a big cast with a sizeable lure if the bale arm flicks over in mid-cast). When lure fishing or float fishing at distance braid definitely makes hooking fish much more reliable.

There has been a tendency in recent years for manufacturers of monofil to produce lines in vivid 'dayglo' fluorescent colours. As far as I can see, the only advantage is that the angler can see the line and its direction easily. It seems to me that the fish will probably see the line better as well and I have always assumed that the less the fish sees of fishing tackle, other than the part designed to be ingested, the better. Therefore I cannot see any real advantage to high-visibility lines for hooking fish. To put it bluntly I wouldn't advise them for any angling purpose (but it might do some good if mono-nets for catching bass were made of this line; I suspect they would catch less fish!).

Sinkers

Tackle has become more and more sophisticated. Even the humble sinker now comes in many shapes and sizes with 'space age' contraptions and extensions. Thankfully the bass angler can cheerfully ignore these refinements. With the change in law regarding small 'leads' it has become difficult to obtain small (1oz or less) weights made out of lead metal and zinc has been used instead. These new sinkers, in the form of drilled bullets, are a menace, because they wear through fishing lines, being much harder than lead itself. Those anglers who are forced to buy 'Zinkers' would be well advised to use heavier line where it runs through the weight if they are to avoid breakages.

Finally, I have recently returned to one of my old fishing habits, which I did not mention in the first edition. In areas without a fast current I use stones with holes in instead of leads when fishing over foul ground. They are much less likely to get stuck and are perfectly effective. A walk along many beaches will provide plenty of stones with holes in, which can be tied onto the chosen rig. I tie some heavy line to the stone and put a loop in the free end; the loop can easily be used to incorporate the sinker into the desired end tackle. I am not kidding you – try it!!

The Mighty Chug Bug

Some members of B.A.S.S. (The Bass Anglers Sportfishing Society) have popularised the use of surface-fished 'popping' lures for bass; in particular the Storm Chug Bug has achieved almost cult status. Probably the most skilled and experienced in the use of these lures are Steve Butler with his pal Mike Hughes. I had already experimented with Chug Bugs, but was fortunate enough to have the benefit of expert guidance from Steve Butler and Paul Nettleton on their home patches in North Wales, areas that I once fished regularly but now fish only very rarely. After catching a few fish in Wales, I have used Bugs to catch fish from several local venues in Devon, and I am sure they would be effective in most places. Certainly Mike (Ladle) was a very easy convert when I was able to show him how to catch bass with them on his own stretch of the Dorset coast (see Mike's piece).

It is a revelation when you first use surface-fished lures. The attack by the fish is visible and very exciting, and the method is quite different from the simple cast and retrieve. These lures can be fished over water of any depth and the snaggiest of ground is no threat to lure loss (until a fish is hooked). The best line to use is a

Bass member Allan Hughes leans into a good fish taken on a Chug Bug.

non-stretch braided one. There are many braids on the market and some are better than others. Some seem more prone to fail when under sudden strain and others are subject to inextricable tangles. Two that seem to be more reliable are 'Fireline' and 'Powercable'.

After casting out the lure, it is retrieved slowly, by a series of sharp tugs which spray water violently over the surface, these are punctuated by longer pauses (up to ten seconds or more) and small twitches, during which a fish may take the lure or show itself on the surface. An attack can come at any time, from the first 'chug' or even from when the lure first hits the water until the moment you lift the lure from under the rod tip. The golden rule is never to strike until you actually feel the fish.

My first Bug-caught bass was a two-pounder that took the lure under the rod tip at first light. My second was after I missed a spectacular take from a bass that hurled itself out of the water and I struck too soon – I couldn't help myself at the time – which taught me the golden rule.

On one occasion I was able to watch the behaviour of fish approaching both large and small Bugs while I was looking down from a rock into clear water. As soon as the chugging began, the fish came to 'have a look' (I saw up to a dozen at a time). With continued chugging, one or more started to attack the lure in earnest and often got hooked. At this place I found that the fish did not move far from their resting 'lies', which seemed to be under and near rock ledges, and returned to them after following the Bug for a while. Sometimes however, bass will follow these lures for considerable distances and can be seen 'stalking' the lure, following and moving round the lure during chugging before taking or rejecting it.

The second golden rule of surface fishing is that, if you detect a fish near your lure, you must leave the lure where it is and just twitch it, rather than retrieve it with long pulls. This fits in with my observation of the fish mentioned above. However, in Devon I have seen fish try to take a lure repeatedly after chugs. In September, in a roughish sea, over shallow rocks, I had five attacks to a bug on successive 'chugs'; it could have been the same fish. I did not catch that fish, but took one on the next cast.

I have now taken bass on Bugs in flat calm and rough conditions, but it is a lot easier and more exciting when calm, clear water means that you can see fish or signs of fish (swirls and so on) more easily.

I have also spoken to another Devonian angler who retrieves his bugs much faster and more or less continuously and has taken bass to 8lb-plus in this way.

Steve B. prefers calm clear water for this method of fishing and he has taken large numbers of bass by using these surface lures, including several over 10lb; he is quite convinced that the Big Bug selects for the bigger fish.

One very startling revelation to me was the fact that surface-fished popping lures work just as well in fast tide races over deep water. Steve B. and I had fished a rocky mark from dawn and I was pleased to have caught two bass on a big Bug, both of which were returned. When we later fished a headland with a fast tide rip over deep water I was expecting sub-surface lures to outfish the poppers. However, although I took another bass on a sub-surface plug Steve fished on with confidence using a big Bug and caught three bass, all of them bigger than mine! It is clear that bass will come up to the surface in deeper water to take poppers.

213

Alan helps Allan Hughes to unhook his 'bug caught' fish.

I have no hesitation in recommending the use of surface lures of the Chug Bug type to keen bass anglers. I am certainly no expert in their use, but my progress has been rapid and I am sure that any angler who persists with these lures will surely be rewarded.

Jerk Baits

Steve Butler has also successfully used jerk baits for bass, particularly in areas where the current is very fast or conditions are too rough for practical use of surface lures.

Pike anglers have been fishing jerk baits for some time and they are essentially fishy-looking imitations, usually of wood or plastic but sometimes of softer materials. These one-piece lures are designed to sink slowly in a horizontal position and have no action of their own until jerked by the angler using a (stiffish) rod.

Steve has made his own jerk baits by removing the lips from diving plugs and adding weight. The crucial feature is to ensure that they sink slowly on an even keel. He has taken good bass on jerk baits and if he uses these lures with the intelligence and persistence he has employed with his other lure fishing, I am sure that he'll do well. Watch this space!

Reflections

It was about 9pm on a dark and warm October evening when I parked the car and walked to a local beach to use live sandeels on the early flood of a spring tide. I knew from past trips that conditions were good with a light surf rolling into the beach, slightly stirring up the bottom. Exactly how bass find live eels in the pitch black it is difficult for us to be sure but find them they do. As well as using sight, smell and the lateral line sense enable bass to locate and take the lively little bars of silver at night.

As I waded into the tide to get fresh sea water in the deep bucket that contained the eels I could see in the torch beam that I was disturbing sand eels, which darted away in the shallows. I had emptied out the water taken from my tank (the bucket had been aerating with a portable pump in the car) and a quick scoop put enough water into the bucket without losing any bait.

I had tackled up with a one-and-a-half-ounce lead running on 12lb mono tied to a small swivel with an 8lb trace of about a yard long. The eels were quite big (about a BIC ballpoint and a half long I remind myself as I write this) and a short-shanked 4/0 hook (Mustad pattern 496B) was tied on. The best way to hook a live eel for casting is straight through the eye sockets from one side to the other; the barb on this hook prevents the eel from escaping.

Having baited up I waded in to lob the bait about 30yd out and beyond the closest wave. I retreated back onto dry sand and adjusted my position so that the line entered the water at right angles to the waters edge and I held the 11ft spinning rod low with the line resting on the beach. Holding the line over my index finger I could feel the tackle move slowly over the bottom and again adjusted my position to keep the line just off tight.

Shortly after casting I felt a light tug-tug and then slack. When you get this type of bite it is better to retreat rather than reel so I moved backwards to regain contact. I could feel another set of tugs, as the bass was moving with the bait, but this time the line tightened as the fish moved away. I lifted the rod and backed up the beach striking at the same time.

This was a good fish and it bent the rod well taking some line and head shaking about 50yd away from me. I struck again as hard as I could with a finger on the spool and settled down to retrieve line. As this bass approached the shallows it went wild and ran out

Alan with a beautiful 7lb 14oz fish taken on a legered, live sandeel.

to sea; I let it go, hoping that the hook was in past the barb. If a bass is well hooked on a snag-free beach it can be played to a stand-still if necessary and there is no rush.

I enjoyed feeling the power of this fish and the rod was well bent into the bass all the time as I pulled it back into the shallows for a second time. I could just make out a splash in front of me and held the line as a wave retreated, grounding the fish. I rushed out to lift the fish to safety and was pleased to see a bass of about 7lb lying on the sand with the hook through the corner of the mouth and the eel, now dead, well up the trace. I do not feel guilty about keeping the occasional fish and I like eating bass, so I decided to kill this one and carried it up to the bait bucket and waterproof tackle box that I use for this type of fishing.

After killing the fish I baited up again and cast out another decent-sized eel. Shortly afterwards I caught another bass of about 5lb, which I returned, and a bit later still hooked but lost a bigger fish in the shallows, which shows just how important it is to strike hard. Often you find yourself bent into a fish that takes line but you can forget in the heat of the moment, especially if using a light rod, that the hook may only be in by the point and a bass mouth is hard in places, so you really must whack the hook in hard during a moment of control.

A bit later the tide went dead and there were no more bites. After a couple of hours fishing and after reviving the eels several times with more water I packed up and returned home to put the remaining eels into my tank. It was interesting to note the stomach contents of the bass I kept: there were seven shore crabs, one flounder and one sole.

As I think back about this night and look through my diary I can remember other fascinating nights with sandeels, including the loss of a really big fish that only Phil, my brother in law, saw as it eluded the net on a steeper beach. Although these superb baits work well in the light I prefer using sandeels in the dark when there is more chance of privacy. It is now several years since I used live eels from the shore and my recent years have been dedicated to lure fishing, but I guess that is one of the pleasures of bass fishing: you can enjoy it in so many ways. I have spent almost entire seasons using only one method, like lure fishing, float fishing with live prawns, legering live sandeels as well as my old favourite method of using big deadbaits for the bigger fish.

At the moment I am still in a lure fishing year and will be fishing for this season's bass number eighty next trip out. I've beached ten bass over that magic ten pounds on bait but I still dream about my first 'double' on a lure. *I guess I'll always be hooked on bass.*

Index